T0294619

Making Cents
Out of Knowledge
Management

Edited by
Jay Liebowitz

THE SCARECROW PRESS, INC.
Lanham, Maryland • Toronto • Plymouth, UK
2008

SCARECROW PRESS, INC.

Published in the United States of America
by Scarecrow Press, Inc.
A wholly owned subsidiary of
The Rowman & Littlefield Publishing Group, Inc.
4501 Forbes Boulevard, Suite 200, Lanham, Maryland 20706
www.scarecrowpress.com

Estover Road
Plymouth PL6 7PY
United Kingdom

British Library Cataloguing in Publication Information Available

Library of Congress Cataloging-in-Publication Data

Liebowitz, Jay, 1957–
  Making cents out of knowledge management / Jay Liebowitz [editor].
    p. cm.
  Includes bibliographical references.
  ISBN-13: 978-0-8108-6048-3 (pbk. : alk. paper)
  ISBN-10: 0-8108-6048-1 (pbk. : alk. paper)
  1. Knowledge management—Economic aspects. 2. Intellectual capital. 3. Social
networks. 4. Organizational learning. 5. Knowledge management—Economic
aspects—Case studies. I. Title.

HD30.2.L527 2008
658.4'038—dc22   2007043225

∞™ The paper used in this publication meets the minimum requirements of
American National Standard for Information Sciences—Permanence of Paper
for Printed Library Materials, ANSI/NISO Z39.48-1992.
Manufactured in the United States of America.

DEDICATION

To the knowledge-sharing community—making the world a better place.

To my wonderful family, friends, students, contributors of this book, and colleagues (at Johns Hopkins University, Scarecrow Press, and here and abroad)—we would be ineffective if we didn't share our knowledge.

Contents

Preface

"Another book?" people asked me.

"Yes," I replied, "this concise, easy-to-read book is needed in the marketplace to provide better guidance on the value and importance of knowledge management for organizations."

"Who should care?" they said.

"This impacts any organization, whether in government, industry, or not-for-profit. With the baby boomer generation nearing retirement, knowledge management should play a key role in an organization's human capital strategy, workforce development, knowledge retention, and succession planning activities."

"Don't most people know this already?" they asked.

"You would be surprised," I responded. "Part of the challenge is that they may not have some of the underlying knowledge to show the value-added benefits of knowledge management initiatives."

"So does your book highlight this area?" they wondered.

"I hope so. The focus is on demonstrating ways to show the value of knowledge in organizations and discussing methods to measure—or make 'cents' (sense) out of—knowledge management outcomes. Furthermore, having representative cases of how organizations have been doing this, from leading practitioners and educators worldwide, reinforces these concepts."

"Sounds like quite a novel and worthwhile endeavor," they said as they started to see the light. "This is quite encouraging."

I have always said that in a given lecture or presentation if you can learn one or two new things that you can readily apply in your organization, then the talk was worthwhile. I hope that this book provides at least a few knowledge nuggets to help organizations deal with the ongoing human capital challenges through using knowledge management approaches. Enjoy!

I

CONCEPTS

1

Knowledge

Today's Valuable Commodity

Jay Liebowitz

THE PREAMBLE

Remember learning about the classical factors of production: land, labor, and capital goods? As we have moved from the Agricultural, Industrial, Information, and Knowledge Ages into today's Intangible Economy, other factors have been added to the traditional production factors, namely, information and now "knowledge and intangibles." Today's organizations are using knowledge as a value differentiator in maximizing their potential—so much so that the Financial Accounting Standards Board (FASB) Statement 142 "addresses how intangible assets that are acquired individually or with a group of other assets (but not those acquired in a business combination) should be accounted for in financial statements upon their acquisition"(p. 1).

Simply put, knowledge and other intangibles are valuable commodities for organizations. In looking at the graying workforce in the United States as the baby boomers near retirement age, a knowledge bleed effect may likely result. This brain drain is a key reason why organizations are developing human capital strategies, whereby knowledge management (KM) is an integral part of their succession planning and workforce development efforts. This "lost" knowledge, as described in David DeLong's book, *Lost Knowledge: Confronting the Threat of an Aging Workforce* (2004), is confronting industry, government, and not-for-profits in the United States and

abroad. Anecdotally, when chief executive officers are asked what distinguishes his or her company from others, they will typically say "It's our people—that's our competitive edge." So, finding ways to capture, harness,
leverage, and share this knowledge within the organization is critical before
the employees leave or retire from the organization.

The "how" and "why" questions lend themselves to "knowledge,"
whereas the "who," "what," "where," and "when" questions may be
thought of as either data or information. Many organizations haven't captured the "decision-making process" and the rationale behind why certain
decisions were made, especially strategic ones. This type of knowledge is
important to retain so that when faced with a similar decision again, there
will be a history of what the important components were, both pros and
cons, in reaching the previous decision on which to base the new decision.
In this manner, the new decision that the organization must make can have
a stronger foundation because the decision maker will be more informed
from analyzing the audit trail of how previous related decisions were made.
Of course, the context for this new decision and various environmental and
internal factors may be different from those in previous related decisions,
but at least the decision maker can learn from these situations.

The knowledge management process of capturing, sharing, and applying
knowledge should hopefully lead to creating knowledge. This process
should act as a catalyst in increasing innovation in the organization. Additionally, social networking (both face-to-face and online) can also enable
the knowledge-sharing process to take place. As I discussed in *Social Networking: The Essence of Innovation* (2007), the ability to meet friends and
"friends of friends" can dramatically increase one's ability to stimulate new
ideas and innovate.

KNOWLEDGE FLOWS IN ORGANIZATIONS

Knowledge flow in organizations has been an important topic, especially as
related to the growing knowledge management field (Ramsey and Levitt
2005). Madsen et al. (2002) look at the dynamics of knowledge flows in
terms of human capital mobility, knowledge retention, and change. They
found that an increased reliance on past experience reduces how much human capital a firm imports in the future. They also showed that inflows of
human capital decline when an organization has recently adopted novel
changes in its operations.

Murphy (2003) wrote his dissertation on preserving intellectual capital in
aging civil service organizations. Murphy found that within medium-size
civil service organizations, face-to-face knowledge transfer was a decided

preference, even when other forms of well-established explicit knowledge transfer conduits were available.

In Norway, a three-year project (2003–2005) titled the "Norwegian National Initiative for Senior Workers" (2005) examined how best to leverage the knowledge of senior employees in the National Insurance Service (under the Ministry of Social Affairs). They examined various activities for cross-generational sharing of knowledge and experience, such as: systematic junior-senior workers having lunch together, apprentice manuals describing areas of learning to be introduced to new employees, and a good practice manual developed locally.

In Canada, Konverge (2003) examined knowledge network mapping for human resources decision support. That study looked at replacement planning in public service organizations, and essentially applied social network analysis (Liebowitz 2006a, 2006b, 2007). Oltra (2005) examined the role of human resources management in terms of knowledge management effectiveness. Gomes-Casseres et al. (2006) explored whether alliances promote knowledge flows. They found that knowledge flows between alliance partners are greater than flows between pairs of nonallied firms, and less than flows between units within single firms. Yamin and Otto (2004) examined the influence of inter- and intraorganizational knowledge flows on innovative performance in multinational enterprises. They found that benefits can be accrued from the integration of dispersed knowledge assets to facilitate efficient innovation. Dahl and Pedersen (2004), in their study of knowledge flows in industrial clusters, found that informal contacts represent an important channel of knowledge diffusion. Nissen (2006) has also examined the role of knowledge dynamics in organizations.

Studies performed by Krackhardt and Hanson (1993) showed that understanding informal networks could increase the influence of managers. If the managers learned who possessed power in networks and how various coalitions functioned, they could work with the informal organization to get work done more efficiently. One study (Assimakopoulos and Macdonald 2002) also revealed that formal collaboration networks emerge out of informal networks, rather than vice versa [15].

In any organization, according to social network theorist Karen Stephenson (Kleiner 2002), there are at least six core layers of knowledge, each comprises its own informal network of people. These six layers are work network, social network, innovation network, expert knowledge network, career guidance/strategic network, and learning network. Everybody exists in all the networks, but different people play different roles in each; a central connector in one may be a boundary spanner in another. Research has shown that employees who are central connectors learn faster, perform better, and are more committed to the organization. These employees are also less likely to leave the company. On the other hand, employees with low centrality, those who are on the periphery, have much higher turnover rates (Krebs 1998). It is vital for managers to recognize these different role players to maximize the productivity.

While sharing of explicit knowledge, which can be easily codified, can be transferred indirectly through various technologies (e.g., email), sharing of complex tacit knowledge through the informal networks requires direct interaction between two or more individuals. A direct tie with the knowledge source(s) must be established and trust must be built (Ford 2003, Roberts 2003). Trust plays an important role in knowledge sharing (Ford 2003). It is frequently commented that in order for people to be willing to share their knowledge, they must have trust (e.g., Wang and Rubenstein-Montano 2003). The study performed by Politis (2003) suggested that trust is essential in the process of strengthening collaboration and knowledge sharing between members of self-managing teams in particular. On the other hand, it is also said that the sharing of information also increases the level of trust (Politis 2003). In other words, as one shares information and knowledge with another individual, the perceived trust increases between these individuals. Managers can create the environments in which trust can be increased by encouraging employees to share knowledge. They cannot, however, force trust to occur (Politis 2003). One easy way to improve the level of trust, anytime and anywhere, is simply to increase the speed with which people respond to communication.

By moving power to the edges of organizations, leveraging shared awareness and dynamic knowledge, and unbundling hierarchical processes, the edge organization aims at creating an efficient self-organization with self-synchronizing capability (Alberts and Hayes 2003). In an edge organization, every member is required to make decisions. Decision making is no longer the responsibility of central command and top-level management. The knowledge flow and business processes in an edge organization are dynamic and synchronized rather than prescribed and sequential (Alberts and Hayes 2003).

MacKinnon (2005) used the term "Knowledge Chain Management" to describe the knowledge flow within an organization. "The knowledge is derived from information (created) and combined with other knowledge (manufactured and socialized), demanded (ordered and externalized) and produced (developed and internalized), inventoried as any physical good and delivered (distributed and refined)" (2005, 1). Then, based on the related costs and benefits, the organization can design the flow of knowledge that will best suit its future needs.

Moreover, an edge organization, according to Gavrieli and Scott (2005), relies highly on constant, real-time interactions and exchange of information, which require high levels of trust. However, due to the dynamic nature of edge organizations, with temporary groups and people of diverse backgrounds, it is difficult to cultivate trust in such environments. Gavrieli and Scott summarized that knowledge flows between similar entities are more efficient than those between dissimilar entities. They believed that trust is the way to mediate this relationship. Thus, the efficiency of knowledge flows in an organization is greatly dependent on the trust created and managed in that organization.

The U.S. Department of Defense is seeking the possibility of reconstructing the command-and-control concept in military organizations. The purpose is to improve the military organization's responsive time and actions (i.e., agility) while facing soaring security threats. Alberts and Hayes (2003) proposed that the military should adopt the "Power to the Edge" approach to reengineer the military organizational architecture and to form an agile edge organization. Furthermore, to stimulate edge organizations, cross-generational knowledge flows (Liebowitz 2004) must be fostered for the survival of these edge organizations.

Nissen (2006) summarizes some key principles of knowledge flows and knowledge dynamics that should be followed. Some of the relevant principles are:

1. Shuttling information around via computers, networks, reports, and communications does not address the flow of knowledge, at least not directly or on the same time scale.
2. Knowledge clumps need to be identified and knowledge flows need to be enabled throughout the organization.
3. Knowledge managers may benefit from an emphasis on tacit knowledge flows.
4. Understanding the kinds of knowledge that are important in an organization's particular environment is essential for promoting the most important knowledge flows.
5. People play the critical role in flows of data, information, and knowledge.
6. Every flow from signal interpretation through knowledge creation requires some kind of knowledge.
7. Changes to workflows demand changes to knowledge flows, and vice versa.
8. Knowledge flows should be planned and managed like workflows are.
9. Knowledge must be put to use through action in order to be useful.
10. Learning both uses and increases knowledge.
11. The impact of KM increases in direct proportion to the reach of knowledge flows through an organization.

Jay Liebowitz

12. Knowledge value analysis provides an approach to measuring the relative value of knowledge associated with various organizational processes.
13. Computational models of knowledge flows provide an approach to mitigating the risk inherent in KM programs.

Tacit knowledge transfer models have been studied to some extent in recent years; however, relatively little has been done as compared with more codified approaches to knowledge management. Certainly, the early work grew out of the Human Resource Accounting (HRA) field, mostly spearheaded by Eric Flamholtz (Flamholtz et al. 2002) at UCLA. In fact, the Office of Naval Research (ONR) was one of the first large organizations to sponsor research dealing with the feasibility of applying HRA to the Navy. Flamholtz's study involved the development and application of a model for measuring the replacement costs of civilian industrial engineers.

Ilovici and Han (2003) developed an organizational knowledge transfer model based on flow rate, conductivity, and drivers. Essentially, the flow rate is proportional to the driving force of the flow and inversely proportional to the resistance of the media the fluid passes through. Foos et al. (2006) studied the factors that influence the transfer of tacit knowledge. Testa (2006), from Italy, wrote a dissertation on the knowledge-transfer process. Lastly, Liebowitz and Simien (2005) have looked at developing a knowledge acquisition methodology for a multi-agent system for sailor assignment.

RETAINING "AT RISK" KNOWLEDGE

Expertise and resulting knowledge flows exist at all levels in the organization. Whether there is a particular administrative process that only a few people know how to do or whether it is being a subject matter expert in a core competency of the organization, expertise exists throughout the organization. Retaining this expertise is vital to an organization's longevity, especially in "at risk" knowledge areas where there isn't a backup expert and the individual who possesses the expertise may be soon retiring from the organization. Additionally, capturing the key knowledge that impacts the strategic mission of the organization is a great necessity.

To assist in this knowledge retention effort, templates for decision rationale and a key-lesson document could be used, as shown in text boxes 1.1 and 1.2. These templates could be populated and made available through web-based knowledge repositories and lessons-learned systems in order to capture some of the decision rationale and successful/bittersweet lessons learned toward building the institutional memory of the organization. In

TEXT BOX 1.1. DECISION RATIONALE TEMPLATE

Decision/Assessment: _____

Prior Knowledge:
(What prior knowledge did you use as related to this decision-making process?)

Factors/Criteria:
(What criteria did you use as part of your decision-making process?)

Alternatives/Strategies:
(What alternatives/strategies did you use?)

Pros/Cons:
(What were the pros and cons of each alternative/strategy?)

What made the decision difficult?

Did you make the right decision? If yes, explain. If no, then what should have been done differently?

**TEXT BOX 1.2. POSSIBLE TEMPLATE
FOR A KEY LEARNING DOCUMENT**

Lesson Info:

- Lesson Number:

- Lesson Date:

- Submitting Organization:

- Submitted by:

- Contact Information:

Lesson Learned Title:

Abstract (2–3 sentences):

Description of Driving Event:

Lesson(s) Learned:

Recommendation(s):

Documents Related to Lesson:

Knowledge Area(s) [Please check all appropriate]:

Impact, Influence, or Leverage of the Lesson Learned:

Approval Info:

- Approval Date:

- Approval Name:

- Approval Organization:

this manner, people will not have to reinvent the wheel and will be able to learn more easily from others' mistakes and successes.

Organizations are using a myriad of approaches for retaining knowledge. Online communities are popular collaboration mechanisms for capturing and sharing knowledge. They typically allow for threaded discussions, posting of documents, question-answer polling, and work flow tasking (if structured as a work group). Lessons-learned and best-practice information systems are also being used to capture and share experiences. The defense, energy, and space industries have been actively using lessons-learned systems for years. The Society for Effective Lessons Learned Sharing (SELLS) has been established for many years within the U.S. Department of Energy agencies and related constituents. Expertise locators and social networking sites have also been quite popular in recent years for making connections between individuals, departments, and organizations. Web-based, online searchable multimedia asset-management systems are also used to capture video nuggets of people's experiences as they tackled various problems related to their work. Knowledge-sharing workshops and knowledge fairs are utilized in various organizations for creating more organizational informal networks and transferring knowledge between more experienced project leaders and up-and-coming ones. Document-management systems and intranet technologies have continued to be used to enable knowledge capture and sharing to take place. Formal phased retirement programs, retiree and alumni associations, and bringing back retirees in various roles are other techniques that organizations are using to help capture, leverage, and share knowledge.

SO WHAT IS THE BOTTOM LINE?

The key message from this chapter is that knowledge is pervasive, and the organizations that are best able to capture, share, apply, and disseminate knowledge will be the survivors. They will be able to become agile learning organizations, making innovation a key part of their business. These "knowledge organizations" are the future of the Knowledge and Intangible Economy in which we live. Knowledge management has a key role to play in order to transform these organizations into "knowledge organizations," and knowledge is the most valuable commodity in today's and tomorrow's world.

REFERENCES

Alberts, D., and R. Hayes. 2003. *Power to the Edge*. CCRP. Available from www .dodccrp.org/publications/pdf/Alberts_Power.pdf.

Assimakopoulos, D., and S. Macdonald. 2002. "A Dual Approach to Understanding Information Networks." *International Journal of Networking and Virtual Organizations* 1 (1).

Dahl, M., and C. Pedersen. 2004. "Knowledge Flows Through Informal Contacts in Industrial Clusters: Myth or Reality?" *Research Policy Journal* 33.

DeLong, D. 2004. *Lost Knowledge: Confronting the Threat of an Aging Workforce*. Oxford: Oxford University Press.

Financial Accounting Standards Board (FASB) 2001. Statement 142. Available from http://72.3.243.42/st/summary/stsum142.shtml.

Flamholtz, E., M. Bullen, and W. Hua. 2002. "Human Resource Accounting: A Historical Perspective and Future Implications," *Management Decision* 40 (10).

Foos, T., G. Schum, and S. Rothenberg. 2006. "Tacit Knowledge Transfer and the Knowledge Disconnect," *Journal of Knowledge Management* 10 (1).

Ford, D. P. 2003. "Trust and Knowledge Management: The Seeds of Success." In C. W. Holsapple (Ed.), *Handbook on Knowledge Management* (Vol. 1). Berlin, Heidelberg: Springer-Verlag.

Gavrieli, D. A., and W. R. Scott. 2005. "Intercultural Knowledge Flows in Edge Organizations: Trust as an Enabler." Available from http://crgp.stanford.edu/publications/working_papers/edgeorgs.pdf.

Gomes-Casseres, B., J. Hagedoorn, and A. Jaffe. 2006. "Do Alliances Promote Knowledge Flows?" *Journal of Financial Economics* 80.

Ilovici, I., and J. Han. 2003. "Optimization of Organizational Knowledge Transfer Model," 16th IEEE Symposium on Computer-Based Medical Systems Proceedings, *IEEE Computer Society* 16.

Kleiner, A. 2002. Karen Stephenson's Quantum Theory of Trust. *Strategy+Business Journal* 29.

Konverge. 2003. *Pilot Project Phase I Report: Knowledge Network Mapping (Using Visualized Network Data for HR Decision Support)*, Toronto, Canada, May.

Krackhardt, D., and J. R. Hanson. 1993. "Informal Networks: The Company behind the Chart." *Harvard Business Review* 71 (4): 104–11.

Krebs, V. E. 1998. "Knowledge Networks: Mapping and Measuring Knowledge Creation and Re-Use." Orgnet.com white paper. Available from www.orgnet.com/IHRIM.html.

Liebowitz, J. 2004. *Addressing the Human Capital Crisis in the Federal Government: A Knowledge Management Perspective*. Burlington, MA: Elsevier/Butterworth-Heinemann.

———. 2006a. *Strategic Intelligence: Business Intelligence, Competitive Intelligence, and Knowledge Management*. New York: Auerbach Publishing/Taylor & Francis.

———. 2006b. *What They Didn't Tell You About Knowledge Management*. Lanham, MD: Scarecrow Press.

———. 2007. *Social Networking: The Essence of Innovation*. Lanham, MD: Scarecrow Press.

Liebowitz, J., and J. Simien. 2005. "Computational Efficiencies for Multi-Agents: A Look at a Multi-Agent System for Sailor Assignment," *Electronic Government: An International Journal* 2 (4).

MacKinnon, D. 2005. "Knowledge as Inventory: Near-Optimizing Knowledge and Power Flows in Edge Organizations," ICCRTS Paper 083, ICCRTS Conference, McLean, VA, June.

Madsen, T., E. Mosakowski, and S. Zaheer. 2002. "The Dynamics of Knowledge Flows: Human Capital Mobility, Knowledge Retention, and Change," *Journal of Knowledge Management* 6 (2).

Murphy, T. 2003. *Controlling Brain Drain: Preserving Intellectual Capital in Aging Civil Service Organizations*, PhD dissertation, Touro University, New York.

National Insurance Service and the Work Research Institute. 2005. Norwegian National Initiative for Senior Workers: English Summary, Oslo, Norway.

Nissen, M. 2006. *Harnessing Knowledge Dynamics: Principled Organizational Knowing and Learning.* London: IRM Press.

Oltra, V. 2005. "Knowledge Management Effectiveness Factors: The Role of HRM." *Journal of Knowledge Management* 9 (4).

Politis, J. D. 2003. "The Connection between Trust and Knowledge Management: What Are Its Implications for Team Performance." *Journal of Knowledge Management* 7 (5).

Ramsey, M. S., and R. E. Levitt. 2005. "A Computational Framework for Experimentation with Edge Organizations." Proceedings International Command & Control Research, Symposium, McLean, VA. Available from www.nps.navy.mil/gsois/cep/docs/2005/Ramsey-Levitt-ICCRTS2005.pdf.

Roberts, J. 2003. "Trust and Electronic Knowledge Transfer." *International Journal of Electronic Business* 1 (2).

Testa, G. 2006. *The Spread of Knowledge: The Importance of Knowledge Transfer Processes.* Dissertation, Universita degli Studi di Napoli Parthenope, Italy.

Wang, R., and B. Rubenstein-Montano. 2003. "The Value of Trust in Knowledge Sharing." In *Knowledge Management: Current Issues and Challenges*, ed. Elayne Coakes. London: IRM Press.

Yamin, M., and J. Otto. 2004. "Patterns of Knowledge Flows and MNE Innovation Performance." *Journal of International Management* 10.

2

Harnessing Knowledge through Knowledge Management

Jay Liebowitz

Look at the numbers: According to Vickie Elmer's article "Well Shy of Retiring" in the *Washington Post* (2007), the Bureau of Labor Statistics reports that the number of workers age fifty-five and older will account for nearly 25 percent of all U.S. jobs in 2020 (currently, the percentage is 16.3 percent), and the workers under age twenty-four will decline to about 13 percent in 2050 (now about 15 percent of the labor force). The U.S. workforce is certainly graying, and this can be seen in local, state, and federal government, as well as in certain industries.

Whether through retirement, attrition, or movement to different groups in the organization, knowledge can quickly vanish in an organization. One particular division at the Internal Revenue Service in Washington, D.C., for example, is concerned about the large number of retirement-eligible senior executives and managers in their division. They have started a knowledge retention and succession planning program to try to capture and share critical knowledge before it walks out the door. The knowledge drain or knowledge bleed effect might be reduced if people opt to stay longer in the workforce; however, knowledge gaps can certainly result if proper workforce development and succession planning are not conducted and thoughtfully formulated in advance.

So, what is the solution? Knowledge management (KM) can be part of the puzzle for dealing with knowledge loss in organizations. This chapter will provide some further background on this subject.

KNOWLEDGE LOSS:
WHAT KNOWLEDGE IS WORTH RETAINING?

If we explore various types of knowledge, we can describe knowledge in terms of strategic, relationship, process, expert, and other types. Strategic knowledge refers to the knowledge that directly relates to the strategic decision making of the organization. Relationship knowledge deals with "who knows who" types of knowledge, as opposed to the traditional "expert" or "who knows what" type of knowledge. Process knowledge refers to the business processes of the organization that may need to be captured.

Each of these types of knowledge has key reasons for being retained. For example, strategic knowledge may emanate from the chief executive officer or Strategic Planning Department in the organization. In order for the organization to achieve its strategic vision, mission, and goals, strategic knowledge will need to be transferred throughout the organization so that "everyone is on the same page." This should help toward allowing the business decisions to be properly aligned with the strategic mission of the organization. In the same manner, relationship knowledge is essential for promoting the informal social networks that exist to accomplish the needed work in the organization. Being able to know who to go to for answers to certain questions is a valuable type of knowledge in the organization. Very few people in the organization may know the "go-to" persons who can answer their questions. Similarly, certain process knowledge and process flows can facilitate running a smoother organization, enabling processes to be better understood by those in the organization. Expert knowledge or "subject matter domain expertise" needs to flourish as well in the organization in order to help add the secret ingredients to the company's formula for success.

Knowledge is typically thought about in the active sense, but it can also become quite stale. Some knowledge can outlive its useful life and may be outdated. For example, there may be a better approach or process for performing a task that would render the predecessor knowledge useless. Whole milk, red meat, and eggs were key parts of the recommended diet forty years ago. With medical advances, we have discovered that this knowledge is no longer valid.

Let's look at a typical scenario in a multinational enterprise that shows the need for better management of knowledge for organizational effectiveness and efficiency.

A TYPICAL SITUATION IN A MULTINATIONAL ORGANIZATION

"I can't seem to find the right document or the right person to speak with!" Sally exclaims. "We have all these different versions of our financial, legal, grantee, and other reports and documents on our shared drive and on our own personal hard drives, which makes it difficult to quickly access the right information at the right time we need it. Additionally, we use Lotus Notes at headquarters and Outlook/Exchange in the affiliates, and everyone prefers the look of their own system. We want to have a seamless integration process, so we don't have to be in our email system, and then go to the document management system, and then move to Word or Excel, and so on. We would love to have a one-stop shopping system with native integration of software packages within the document management system, as well as having the capability to create, store, search, and retrieve documents in at least English, Spanish, and Russian. It would be great to be able to even search on videos or webcasts that may be part of the repository, and have ways to automatically tag and dynamically develop the taxonomy for labeling/searching all types of documents (and images). Having some visualization techniques to better display searches and clusters of documents, and for helping the user navigate through the 150,000+ documents would be extremely helpful. Also, an ability to store lessons learned and best practices would be needed, and having capabilities to capture the tacit knowledge that we have would be very useful." Sally takes a deep breath of air.

"And that is only for the document management piece of our knowledge management solution," Sally points out. "We also want to be able to develop online communities and expertise locator systems across our worldwide regions, hubs, affiliates, and HQ, with about 1,000 users. Of course, part of the challenge is the varying degree of Internet connectivity in some of these remote parts of the world—even using 28 baud hook-ups. The collaboration part of our KM approach could perhaps give us the most impact in terms of sharing information and knowledge across online communities, similar to what the World Bank and other organizations have used. But we thought we would start with the document management system component of our KM strategy as a low-hanging fruit."

Is this situation described above really that far-fetched? In today's fast-changing knowledge economy, many multinational organizations face similar challenges. Finding the answers to "who knows what," "who knows who," "how to do this," and "why are we doing this" is often a difficult task. In this regard, knowledge management may be able to be a savior.

When we speak of knowledge management, we are trying to best leverage knowledge internally in the organization and externally to stakeholders and customers. We are interested in creating value out of the intangible assets in the organization. In the previous situation, Sally is expressing the need to better capture, share, apply, and disseminate knowledge, whether tacit (in the heads of individuals) or explicit (codified). This is essentially the knowledge management process, with the end result being the creation of knowledge. Through knowledge creation, organizations will innovate to produce new products and services. KM also offers the advantages of build-ing the institutional memory of the organization and developing a stronger sense of belonging and community in the organization. It also helps to es-tablish a stronger bond between the customers and the organization, as in the case of Hallmark having online communities to get ideas for new greet-ing cards from Hallmark customers.

THE BUILDING BLOCKS OF KNOWLEDGE MANAGEMENT

Knowledge is the capability to act—actionable information. When we speak of data, we refer to discerned elements. If we pattern the data, we may pro-duce information. When we make information actionable, then we gener-ate knowledge.

A wonderful story that helps define knowledge can be told as follows:

> A fellow walks into a bank in Manhattan, and tells the loan officer that he needs a loan for $2,000 to take a two-week trip to Europe. The loan officer asks, "What kind of collateral do you have?" The man replies, "You see that Rolls Royce out front. That's my car and here are my car keys."
>
> The man gets the loan, and comes back two weeks later to see the loan offi-cer for repayment of his loan. He asks the loan officer, "How much do I owe you?" The loan officer replies, "It's $2,000 plus $15.46 for interest. And by the way, we checked into your records and noticed that you are a multimillionaire. Why did you need to get a loan for just $2,000?" The man replies, "Where else could you park for two weeks in New York City for only $15.46!"

In this vignette, this gentleman applied his "knowledge." He made his money work for him and put the information gained into action. Today's and future C-level executives will also have to be successful in translating infor-mation into knowledge. Many organizations have hired chief knowledge of-ficers, chief learning officers, knowledge management officers, intellectual capital directors, and the like to help the organization apply knowledge man-agement principles for developing a human-capital strategy for workforce de-velopment and succession-planning purposes. In the U.S. federal govern-ment, the chief human capital officer's position was created in 2003 to help the largest U.S. agencies and departments create a human capital strategy for the organization, especially with the aging workforce demographics.

Toward developing a human-capital strategy, there should be at least four major pillars supporting it. One pillar is competency management—what are the competencies needed in the organization's workforce of the future? The second is performance management—how will the organization recog-nize and reward individuals based on performance, or provide disincentives for lack of performance? The third key pillar is change management—how does the organization create a culture that can be adaptive and agile to handle change? And the fourth pillar is knowledge management.

Most people will agree that knowledge management has four major processes: knowledge identification and capture, knowledge sharing, knowledge application, and knowledge creation. This closely follows the SECI model—socialization, externalization, combination, and internalization. Key types of knowledge are identified and captured (socialization), shared (socialization and externalization), and applied (combination), resulting in new knowledge (internalization). This new knowledge then goes through the knowledge management process again to be captured, shared, and applied to hopefully spawn other knowledge.

Most KM practitioners believe that there are three major components of knowledge management: people/culture, process, and technology. The people/culture part looks at how to create and nurture a knowledge-sharing environment in the organization. The process part examines how to embed knowledge management processes within the daily working lives of the employees. The technology component is how to create a unified knowledge network to enable knowledge sharing to take place. There is usually an 80–20 rule, whereby the 80 percent of KM deals with people/culture and process, and the other 20 percent is the technology piece. The toughest part is to change the "knowledge is power" culture to a "sharing knowledge is power" paradigm. Changing the organization's recognition and reward structure to encourage knowledge sharing is often part of the knowledge management strategy.

In order for knowledge management to be successful in an organization, several critical success factors should be achieved. The knowledge management strategy should be directly aligned with the strategic mission of the organization. Senior leaders should also be committed to the knowledge management initiatives in terms of moral and financial involvement. And knowledge-sharing tenets should also be woven within the fabric of the organization in order to integrate across the functional silos in most organizations. These tenets may be:

- Learn from others so that you don't have to reinvent the wheel.
- Build a continuous learning environment, which entails learning from both successes and failures and being encouraged to share what you know, especially the bittersweet tales.
- Think often of "we" versus "I."
- Incorporate learning and knowledge-sharing proficiencies within the annual employee performance review.
- Most people like to be recognized, versus strictly being rewarded.
- Build your informal network within the organization in order to maximize performance.

CONDUCTING A KNOWLEDGE AUDIT

In the same manner that manufacturers take an inventory of their physical assets, organizations need to do the same with their intellectual capital or knowledge assets. This is one of the first steps that should be done in order for an organization to develop its knowledge management strategy. We call this process a "knowledge audit." Most people and organizations don't like the term "audit," so using a euphemism like a "knowledge assessment" or a "knowledge use and sharing study" may suffice.

Most people in the organizations seem to actually enjoy participating in the knowledge audit, as it is something novel for them and allows them to provide input on how to best share and leverage their knowledge internally and externally. The knowledge audit process that is typically applied is:

- After gaining senior management approval to conduct the knowledge audit, a "knowledge assessment and sharing" survey is developed to look at a number of areas such as respondent demographics (like department and tenure in the organization), knowledge resources, knowledge sharing and use, training/tools and knowledge needs, and knowledge flows. The survey, as shown in figure 2.1, is refined iteratively in working with the organization, and is then put in a web-based format using SurveyMonkey (www.surveymonkey.com) or some other web-based survey tool.
- The survey is then piloted within the organization to a selected representative set of respondents and further refined before being sent to the masses.
- The senior manager or champion in the organization who promotes the knowledge audit then sends an email to alert everyone about the survey and why it is being conducted. Confidentiality is also preserved as indicated in the survey.
- The survey is then made "live" in the web-based format, and a two-week completion date is typically set.
- Before, during, and after the survey, interviews and/or focus groups are conducted by the knowledge audit team across a representative set of organizational members. The interviews help to shape the survey, as well as allow more detail and clarity for better understanding the survey results.
- A report on the knowledge audit results and the resulting knowledge management strategy is written and presented to the knowledge audit sponsors. A briefing is also conducted to the organization on the knowledge audit results and KM strategy.

Figure 2.1. Knowledge Access and Sharing Survey
(Developed by Dr. Jay Liebowitz, JHU)

A key part of developing a knowledge management strategy is to find out how people gain access to and share knowledge throughout the organization. This survey seeks to gather fairly detailed information about the ways in which you access, share, and use knowledge resources in your work. In answering the questions below, please keep in mind the following: answer for yourself, not how you think someone else in your job might answer; answer for how you *actually* work now, not how you wish you worked or think you should work.

We expect that some questions will require you to think carefully about the nature of the tasks you perform and how you interact with people both inside and outside the organization day to day. Carefully completing this survey will probably take about twenty minutes. *We appreciate your effort in helping us meet a strategic goal designed to make the organization more effective and to make it easier for all of us to do our jobs on a daily basis.*

Please forward your completed survey to _____ via email _____ by _____.
Thank you!

PLEASE PROVIDE THE FOLLOWING INFORMATION:

Name: _____

Which division are you a part of: _____

How long have you been a full-time employee in the organization?

❑ Less than 6 months
❑ 6 months – less than 1 year
❑ 1 year – less than 3 years
❑ 3 years – less than 5 years
❑ More than 5 years

PLEASE BEGIN THE SURVEY!

1. In the course of doing your job, which resource do you most often turn to *first* when looking for information? (*please check only one*)

   ❑ Email or talk to a colleague in the organization
   ❑ Email or talk to a colleague who works outside the organization
   ❑ Do a global web search (for example, Google, Yahoo)
   ❑ Go to a known website
   ❑ Search online organization resources (for example, intranet)
   ❑ Search through documents/publications in your office
   ❑ Post a message on a list-serv/online community to which you belong
   ❑ Ask your manager for guidance based on his/her experience
   ❑ Other (*please specify*) _____

2. What would be your second course of action from the above list?

   _____

3. Think about the times when you've been really frustrated by not having a critical piece of knowledge or information you needed to get something done at the organization. Give an example, including the nature of the challenge and how the need eventually was met.

   _____
   _____
   _____

KNOWLEDGE RESOURCES

4. How often **on average** do you use each of the following to do your job?

	DAILY	WEEKLY	MONTHLY	QUARTERLY	NEVER
Organization-wide database	❑	❑	❑	❑	❑
Organization-operated website (e.g., intranet)	❑	❑	❑	❑	❑
Department- or division-operated database (e.g., shared calendar)	❑	❑	❑	❑	❑
My own database or contact list file	❑	❑	❑	❑	❑
Organization policy/ procedures manual or guidelines	❑	❑	❑	❑	❑
Department- or division-specific procedures manual or guidelines	❑	❑	❑	❑	❑
Vendor-provided procedures manual or guidelines	❑	❑	❑	❑	❑

(*continues*)

Figure 2.1. (*continued*)

5. List up to five resources (hard copy or web-based) that you use to perform your job and indicate how often you use them. These resources can be journals, magazines, newsletters, books, websites, and so forth.

	DAILY	WEEKLY	MONTHLY	QUARTERLY
1.	❏	❏	❏	❏
2.	❏	❏	❏	❏
3.	❏	❏	❏	❏
4.	❏	❏	❏	❏
5.	❏	❏	❏	❏

6. How often **on average** do you ask each of the following staff for help with understanding or clarifying how you are to perform your job, solving a problem, getting an answer to a question from a customer, or learning how to accomplish a new task?

	DAILY	WEEKLY	MONTHLY	QUARTERLY	NEVER
Your immediate supervisor	❏	❏	❏	❏	❏
Your department head	❏	❏	❏	❏	❏
Your division head	❏	❏	❏	❏	❏
Subject matter expert (in an area of policy, practice, or research)	❏	❏	❏	❏	❏
Technical or functional expert (e.g., accounting, legal, contracts administration, technology)	❏	❏	❏	❏	❏
A peer or colleague in your department or division (informal)	❏	❏	❏	❏	❏
A peer or colleague outside your department or division (informal)	❏	❏	❏	❏	❏

7. Name the top three people, in order, to whom you go when you have questions or seek advice in the following areas:

	ONE	TWO	THREE
General advice			
Management and leadership knowledge/advice			
Subject matter expertise/content knowledge			
Institutional/historical knowledge about the foundation			
Technical/procedural knowledge			

8. List up to five experts *outside* the organization whom you access to do your job. For each one, please indicate how often **on average** you contact them.

		DAILY	WEEKLY	MONTHLY	QUARTERLY
1.		❏	❏	❏	❏
2.		❏	❏	❏	❏
3.		❏	❏	❏	❏
4.		❏	❏	❏	❏
5.		❏	❏	❏	❏

KNOWLEDGE USE

9. Which of the following do you *usually* use and/or perform (that is, on a daily or weekly basis) in doing your job? (*check all that apply*)

   ❏ Data or information from a known source (e.g., database, files) you have to retrieve to answer a specific question.
   ❏ Data or information you have to gather yourself from multiple sources and analyze and/or synthesize to answer a specific question.
   ❏ Instruction (step-by-step) you provide (that is, not a document) to a customer, vendor, or staff person.
   ❏ Direction you provide to a customer, vendor, or staff person (such as advice, counsel, or guidance, not step-by-step).
   ❏ Judgments or recommendations you are asked to make based on data or information that is given to you.
   ❏ Judgments or recommendations you are asked to make based on data or information that you must find yourself.
   ❏ Routine procedure or process for handling information, paperwork, requests, payments, invoices, and so forth (always done the same way).
   ❏ Variable procedure or process for handling information, paperwork, requests, payments, invoices, and so forth (requires some analysis and judgment to select the proper procedure or process to follow).
   ❏ Reports, memoranda, letters, or informational materials for customers, vendors, or staff that you must compile and/or write.
   ❏ Educational or promotional materials that you must compile and/or write.
   ❏ Proposals you develop to recommend new programs, projects, procedures, or processes.

10. After you have received, gathered, or produced information, instructions, documents, proposals, etc., and completed the task, what do you do with them? (*check all that apply*)

   ❏ Save them in an electronic file in my personal directory
   ❏ Save them in an electronic file in a shared directory (e.g., s:drive, intranet)
   ❏ Save them in a personal paper file
   ❏ Save them in a secure departmental paper file
   ❏ Save them in an open departmental paper file
   ❏ Share them or distribute them to others
   ❏ Delete or toss them
   ❏ Other (*please specify*) _____

(*continues*)

Figure 2.1. (*continued*)

11. When you come across a news item, article, magazine, book, website, announcement for a meeting, or course, or some other information that may be useful to other organization staff, what are you *most likely* to do? (*check only one*)

   ❑ Tell them about it or distribute a copy to them personally
   ❑ Post an announcement on the intranet
   ❑ Send a broadcast email
   ❑ Send a memo or a copy through the interoffice mail
   ❑ Intend to share it but usually too busy to follow through
   ❑ Include it in the Weekly Update
   ❑ Ignore it
   ❑ Other (*please specify*) _____

12. What are the constraints you face in being able to access or share knowledge?

   _____
   _____
   _____
   _____
   _____
   _____

13. What critical knowledge is at risk of being lost in your department or division because of turnover and lack of back-up expertise?

   _____
   _____
   _____
   _____
   _____

TRAINING/TOOLS

14. When you want to learn or improve a skill or task, what do you prefer to do? (*check all that apply*)
   ❑ Get formal face-to-face training or course work outside the work place
   ❑ Get formal self-directed training (e.g., workbook, CD-ROM, online course)
   ❑ Have a specialist train me on-site
   ❑ Train myself (informally, using a manual or tutorial program)
   ❑ Have my supervisor show me how to do it
   ❑ Have a friend or colleague show me how to do it
   ❑ Other (*please specify*) _____

15. What kind of tools or resources do you prefer to help you do your job? (*check all that apply*)

- ❏ Person I can talk to in real time
- ❏ Help line or help desk via phone, fax, or email
- ❏ Advice via online communities of practice (on the intranet, listservs, or other sources)
- ❏ Printed documents (for example, resource books, manuals)
- ❏ Electronic documents
- ❏ Audiovisual/multimedia material
- ❏ Special software
- ❏ Web-based utility, directory, or service
- ❏ Other (*please specify*) _____

KNOWLEDGE NEEDS

16. What information or knowledge that *you* don't currently have would you like to have to do your job better? Consider all aspects of your job, including administrative tasks, policies and procedures, interpersonal relationships, and so forth.

_____
_____
_____
_____
_____
_____
_____
_____

17. What information or knowledge that *the organization* currently does not have do you think it should or will need to have to execute its mission, improve organizational effectiveness, and serve its customers with excellence? (You may answer for specific departments as well as for the organization as a whole.)

_____
_____
_____
_____
_____
_____
_____
_____

(*continues*)

Figure 2.1. (*continued*)

18. To what extent do you agree with the following statements:

	STRONGLY DISAGREE	DISAGREE	NO OPINION	AGREE	STRONGLY AGREE
I would benefit from having access to documents that contain introductory knowledge that I currently have to acquire from experts directly.	❏	❏	❏	❏	❏
I would benefit from templates to help me more easily capture knowledge (e.g., standard format for documenting what I learned at a conference or meeting).	❏	❏	❏	❏	❏
I would benefit from processes to help me contribute knowledge that I don't currently document or share.	❏	❏	❏	❏	❏
I would benefit from support to determine the most relevant knowledge to share for various audiences and how best to share it.	❏	❏	❏	❏	❏
I have knowledge in areas that I know the organization could benefit from but no way to make it available.	❏	❏	❏	❏	❏

KNOWLEDGE FLOW

19. Imagine that you've just won the first organization Knowledge Sharing Award. This award is given to a person who shares his or her mission- or operation-critical knowledge so that the organization can be more effective. List the top five categories of knowledge that earned you this award and the category of staff with whom you shared it.

	KNOWLEDGE CATEGORY	STAFF CATEGORY
1.		
2.		
3.		
4.		
5.		

20. How can the knowledge flow in your area of responsibility be improved?

_____

_____

_____

_____

_____

ADDITIONAL COMMENTS

_____

_____

_____

_____

_____

Thank you for taking the time to complete this survey.

The knowledge audit process described above usually takes about three to four months, depending on the size and geographic dispersion of the organization, with several knowledge audit team members. Techniques like social network analysis can be applied in order to map "who goes to who" for various types of knowledge (strategic, relationship, expert, process, institutional, etc.) inside and outside the organization. Social network analysis tools like NetMiner (www.netminer.com) and NetDraw (www.analytictech.com) can be used to visualize and analyze the results (Liebowitz 2007).

CROSS-GENERATIONAL KNOWLEDGE FLOWS IN ORGANIZATIONS

The tacit knowledge transfer between employees can be affected by their cross-generational biases. These intergenerational differences result from the particular generation in which they were born and the environment in which they live. Those in the "war" generation, baby boomer generation, Generation X, or Generation Y may have different views on life and how this impacts the work environment. This will affect the quality and amount of knowledge that is transferred from one employee to another. Figure 2.2 shows a cross-generational knowledge transfer survey that could be used to determine the effects of inter-generational biases on tacit knowledge transfer.

Figure 2.2. Cross-Generational Knowledge Flow and Sharing Questionnaire

Developed by Dr. Jay Liebowitz and Nirmala Ayyavoo (Johns Hopkins University) and James Simien (NPRST)—Developed Through a Navy Research Contract N00244-07-C-0001

A. What generation were you born?

    _____ "War" generation (1945 or earlier)
    _____ Baby boomers (1946–1965)
    _____ Generation Xers (1966–1979)
    _____ Generation Yers (1980 or later)

B. To what extent do you agree with the following statements?

Statement	Strongly Disagree	Disagree	Neutral	Agree	Strongly Agree
1. I expect the competency of the individuals on my team to be high.					
2. Most of the knowledge that I will contribute to the team will be from my life's experiences.					
3. I believe that there may be generational gaps on our team resulting in different expectations.					
4. I have dedicated work ethics.					
5. I have strong family values.					
6. I enjoy volunteering.					
7. I believe that the whole is greater than the sum of its parts.					
8. Most of the knowledge flows between my team members will be through codified means (e.g., use of blackboard, reports, articles, email, etc.).					
9. I expect that the distribution of knowledge to appropriate individuals on my team will be done actively on a frequent basis.					
10. I have certain biases that may affect my performance on the team.					

Statement	Strongly Disagree	Disagree	Neutral	Agree	Strongly Agree
11. I expect that our team's effectiveness will depend mostly on the knowledge flows between the client and our team.					
12. I know where to go to get the information that I need					
13. The information that I need to make decisions is readily available.					
14. I feel that rotating leaders on project teams inhibits knowledge flows within the team.					
15. I am more collaborative than competitive.					
16. I am willing to share my knowledge with others because I feel they will reciprocate.					
17. I am loyal to the team's mission.					
18. I feel that the project leader should be more knowledgeable than the other team members.					
19. On my team, I expect individual action to be highly valued.					
20. On my team, people will be expected to stick to rules and procedures even when there are better solutions.					
21. I feel that I will be rewarded based upon my ability to share my knowledge with others.					
22. Knowledge is power.					

(continues)

Figure 2.2.   (*continued*)

Statement	Strongly Disagree	Disagree	Neutral	Agree	Strongly Agree
23. Sharing knowledge is power.					
24. I feel informal communications will foster trust and help better share knowledge in a group.					
25. I feel knowledge flows more easily when people of the same gender work as a team.					
26. Appreciation will motivate me to contribute better.					
27. Uncertainty and change can be better dealt with when the size of the team is smaller.					
28. By working together early on, I feel that this should lead to a successful project.					
29. My work and family commitments may constrain my efforts on this project.					

SUMMARY

Now that we have a basic understanding of the importance of knowledge and knowledge management building blocks, we can start to examine some ways to show value from an organization's knowledge management initiatives. The next chapter will look at various metrics, measures, and approaches to help quantify these intangible assets.

REFERENCES

Elmer, Vickie. 2007. "Well Shy of Retiring." *Washington Post*, January 30.
Liebowitz, J. 2007. *Social Networking: The Essence of Innovation*. Lanham, MD: Scarecrow Press, Lanham.

3

Maximizing Value from Knowledge Management

Simple Ways to Get Started

Jay Liebowitz

"Show me! Why should I invest resources into knowledge management in my organization? My outlook today is more near-term, and not the long-term focus that knowledge management has."

This is a typical response that senior management may give with respect to investing in knowledge management initiatives. As evidenced in Sarv Devaraj and Rajiv Kohli's book, *The IT Payoff: Measuring the Business Value of Information Technology Investments* (2002), measuring return on investment (ROI) is always a challenge but is necessary to put management's mind at ease. In the knowledge management world, where intangibles are abundant, some people say that "return on vision" might be effective through serious anecdotal evidence to show the value of KM. However, in this competitive environment, the business case typically has to be presented for why resources should be placed in KM versus other areas. As Grant Jacoby and Luqi (2007) state, "Turning information into knowledge capital that corporations can leverage quickly for competitive advantage requires a model and metrics that tractably support it." Anderson (2002) states, "Measuring intangible assets has been the missing ingredient."

According to "The Insider's Guide to Knowledge Management ROI" (Tobin 2004), the following reasons make a compelling case for measuring ROI of a KM initiative: Benchmarking metrics establishes a baseline, sets expectations, gains management acceptance, creates a repeatable model for measuring success, and recognizes true ROI. Skandia, an international financial services organization, was one of the first corporations to quantify their intangible assets. They developed about 112 metrics to be included in their Intellectual Capital Navigator report. These metrics addressed financial, customer, process, renewal and development, and human capital (Edvinsson and Malone 1997). Sveiby (1997) developed the Intangible Assets Monitor, looking at human competence, internal structure, and external structure (National Electronic Library for Health 2005), and Roos et al. (1998) developed the Intellectual Capital Services' IC Index to measure relationship, human, infrastructure, and innovation capital (National Electronic Library for Health 2005).

Kankanhalli and Tan (2004) review metrics for knowledge management systems and knowledge management initiatives. They found that there is a lack of research on usability of KM systems and limited studies on usage of KM systems. They also discovered that there were three general-purpose approaches to measure the impact of KM initiatives: House of Quality, Balanced Scorecard, and the APQC (American Productivity and Quality Center) KM benchmarking approach.

KM metrics for measuring intellectual capital have been surveyed (Liebowitz and Suen 2000) and fuzzy logic also applied to develop metrics for determining KM success (Liebowitz 2005). This technique lends itself very well to help quantify the soft measures into hard ones. Activity-based valuation has been proposed as a model for human capital (Liebowitz and Wright 1999). Here, activity-based inflows lead to human capital valuation accounting with objective-based amortization outflows.

Kay (2003) feels that knowledge management is simply a critical component and an overhead cost of doing business. In law firms, Kay mentions that measurement of intangible benefits can only be done qualitatively by undertaking partner and lawyer surveys. Martin (2002), however, believes that cost justification could be determined by a formula: cost of information − document preparation cost / rate of reuse. Alber (2004) feels that goals for knowledge management projects should be aligned with the firm's core business model and clients' interests.

Knowledge@Wharton (2001) cites the business value index, scenario planning, and real option theory for how managers and executives can account for intangible value. Gold et al. (2001) show that technology, structure, and culture form a definitional basis for the theoretical framework of social capital. Wickhorst (2002) developed an Intellectual Capital Performance Measurement Model to measure the ROI on knowledge management systems. Over the years, Bontis (2002), Brooking (1996), Lev (2001), Flamholtz (2003), and Housel and Bell (2001) have been actively researching techniques for measuring knowledge management and intangible assets.

PRINCIPLES OF MEASUREMENT

Smith and McKeen (2004) discuss the importance of showing the value of KM initiatives to management. They pose several principles of measurement:

- Pay attention to what is measured.
- There are no silver bullets.
- Business metrics are important.
- Measure at different levels.
- Monitor leading indicators.
- Clarify what "value" means.

With respect to knowledge management, Smith and McKeen (2004) feel that a measurement matrix for managers should answer three key questions:

- How well are we using knowledge now?
- Are we doing the right things with knowledge?
- Are we positioned well to compete with knowledge in the future?

There are some simple approaches to measure the value of KM initiatives. One approach is to look at time and cost savings in terms of process flows before and after the KM initiative is applied in the organization. For example, if it takes you x hours less time to locate a person, knowledge, or information through using the KM system versus the status quo, then the cost savings per hours worked could be easily computed.

Another fairly easy measure is to assess the quality of the knowledge received. That is, what is the value of the knowledge conveyed to the knowledge recipient? Using the knowledge recipient to determine the "worth" of the knowledge transferred, "going down the wrong paths" could be calculated in terms of not using the knowledge conveyed. For example, an organization may have a lesson in their lessons-learned information system that states "certain vibration-testing procedures are likely to damage a satellite during the testing phase." If this advice was not followed and damage to the satellite resulted, then the costs incurred in the delay of the project and the cost of new hardware needed to repair or replace parts of the satellite could be calculated quite easily. Additionally, depending upon the knowledge recipient, the value of the knowledge conveyed may vary. For example, if I already knew the knowledge nugget, then its worth may be diminished as compared with someone who never knew about that piece of knowledge. In this manner, the determination of worth will fluctuate based upon the knowledge recipient.

Smith and McKeen (2004) highlight some possible KM measures by type, as shown below:

Operational Measures

- Portal usage/hits
- Attendance at KM-related events
- Number of downloads
- Anecdotes about successes
- The value achieved by a given project with which KM was associated
- Contributions to the knowledge base
- Number of learning hours
- Hours saved with knowledge tools
- Delivery against the KM action plan
- Questions answered by an online community of practice

Tactical Measures

- Surveys of core competencies
- Findings from the knowledge audit
- Number of people who consult with KM
- Demand for KM
- Response to prototypes
- Trends over time
- Evolution of products and services
- KM's ability to support/facilitate communities

Strategic Measures

- Leadership development through application of KM practices
- Alumni contacts
- Diversity metrics
- Amount of KM consulting done

SERIOUS ANECDOTAL EVIDENCE

Often, in knowledge management, serious anecdotal evidence is used as a way to measure the value of a knowledge management effort. Anecdotal evidence may be in the form of stories or organizational narratives. For example, the World Bank has used storytelling as a powerful way to communicate throughout their membership. By using thematic groups (essentially online communities) at the World Bank, investment projects can learn from other similar investment projects, such as in urban transportation and community development. These thematic groups have been very effective in sharing knowledge so that possible pitfalls can be avoided up front.

The large consulting firms have stressed that their knowledge management systems have helped them develop proposals, in response to a request for proposal, much faster than without consulting a KM system to view similar types of proposals. Of course, these time savings could be equated with dollars to produce some tangible amount of money.

Examples of testimonials, a form of anecdote, are shown below, as related to the Johns Hopkins University Master of Science-Information and Telecommunications Systems for Business capstone projects, which I coordinated:

"Johns Hopkins' capstone project with the Foundation was a complete success. The students dedicated themselves fully to the work, completing an assessment of the Foundation's knowledge management (KM) initiative and benchmarking it against KM programs elsewhere in the Foundation, government, and business world. Their recommendations were relevant and valuable, many of which we have already begun implementing. Congratulations to the School of Professional Studies in Business and Education for such a strong program."

"I'm not quite sure what I initially expected from my participation with your Masters Degree Program Capstone project. I think that I expected a student effort resulting in some interesting but incomplete suggestions—and maybe even a little demo program. My expectations were so far surpassed by the level of interest, expertise, competence and results that I'm at a loss for words! I quickly found that I was working with a true group of Information Technology professionals. These students were not professionals in training; they were strong professionals that I'd love to have working on my team. With expert guidance from the faculty advisor, the students maintained an intense focus on the project and progressed rapidly from investigational research to alternative solutions to prototype design. Attractive alternative solutions such as open source (which we had not even considered prior to the Capstone Project) were investigated. With an overall goal of evaluating replacement alternatives for an antiquated service workload tracking system, the Capstone project resulted in over 400 pages of detailed research; complete documentation of the existing system as well as program specifications for a replacement system; a summary of alternatives from which we could choose a system to best fit our needs; and, perhaps most impressive of all, a functional (and beautifully designed) working prototype system."

"The State agency could not have been more pleased with the results of our participation in the Johns Hopkins University MS-ITS Capstone Project. The Capstone Project Team Members provided us with a step-by-step road-map for establishing the department's web-presence and creating a site that will serve as a comprehensive resource for individuals with disabilities throughout the state. The partnership has proved invaluable; especially when you consider that it would have required our agency to spend much more time and resources to produce the same result."

"The Hotel's Information Resources Application Services Financial Systems department recently engaged the Johns Hopkins University (JHU) School of Professional Studies in Business & Education Information and Telecommunications Systems graduate students to address a technical approach to improve employee job satisfaction within the department. There were several areas to be addressed including skills development (training), inter-departmental communications, solicitation of feedback, and knowledge management and the JHU teams had limited time and information from which to work. The skills and professionalism exhibited by the JHU Graduate students were top-notch and provided this internal project with the physical and intellectual manpower equal if not surpassing that often contracted on externally funded initiatives. The analysis and recommendations far exceeded the expectations of management and the information presented is now being utilized in setting departmental objectives for the coming year. Furthermore, management within the department has expressed an interest in partnering with JHU in future capstone projects."

"The Federal government experience with the Johns Hopkins University Capstone Program has been tremendous. The Program worked closely with the Office over two semesters—each as an outcome of the University's competitive selection process. The outcomes of each semester resulted in valuable "white papers" that more than helped direct the Office's necessary enhancement of its website. Each semester's students were advised by professors who educated the students on the unique challenges and realities of federal government and provided leadership that ensured the positive outcomes."

These testimonials may not necessarily compute to dollars, but they capture the essence of the worth of these projects in the eyes of the capstone sponsors (i.e., clients). Some people claim that perhaps KM should be thought of as "return on vision" versus "return on investment." Certainly, the aforementioned testimonials ascribe to this theory.

LEARNING AND KNOWLEDGE-SHARING PROFICIENCIES

Besides some basic metrics and serious anecdotal evidence, organizations are developing learning and knowledge-sharing proficiencies to incorporate value into their organization through knowledge management practices. By including these proficiencies within the recognition and reward structure, employees will apply knowledge-sharing techniques to further innovate and build the institutional memory of the organization. In a number of organizations, such as the World Bank, these learning and knowledge-sharing proficiencies are part of the employee's annual performance review.

Possible knowledge-sharing proficiencies/competencies could include:

- Intradepartment communications: Communicates well with those within his/her department;

- Interdepartment communications: Communicates effectively with those in other departments;
- Knowledge contribution: Shares knowledge through various knowledge management mechanisms, such as mentoring, conference trip report discussions via brown bag lunches, storytelling (organizational narratives), lessons-learned/best practice content contribution, online communities/ threaded discussions, company newsletter contributions, etc.);
- Collaboration: Actively participates in cross-functional teams;
- Knowledge dissemination: Regularly distributes articles of interest to other employees; and
- Knowledge value: Shows value-added benefits from knowledge received from others and knowledge gained by others; and
- Knowledge creation: Willing to be innovative, take risks, and try new ideas.

Various awards could also be associated with these learning and knowledge-sharing proficiencies to encourage the nurturing of a knowledge sharing culture. A "Significant Learning" award, for example, could be used to recognize people who shared their bittersweet stories with others so that the same mistakes wouldn't be made. Team awards could be given to recognize the collective talents of a project team, thereby encouraging knowledge transfer to take place. Ultimately, intrinsic motivators should be used to trump extrinsic motivators over time. Recognition, as in the case of intrinsic motivators, versus rewards, as in the case of extrinsic motivators, is typically a driver for most employees—they want to be recognized for their talents. Psychological experiments have shown that extrinsic rewards can actually inhibit intrinsic motivation.

COMPETITIVE INTELLIGENCE

Another way to measure the effects of an organization's knowledge management effort is to compare how the organization is doing versus its competitors. Competitor profiling, benchmarking, and industry analyses can provide insight into how the organization is faring with its competitors. Various KM benchmarking studies, such as those done by the APQC, can shed light on best practices used by other organizations in terms of knowledge management efforts. For example, APQC's Consortium Learning Forum's 2003 Best Practice Report on "Measuring the Impact of Knowledge Management" (APQC 2003) of thirty-three organizations indicated the following:

- Measures are appropriate to a particular knowledge management approach, its objectives, and its stage of development.

- APQC's Measurement Framework, which links inputs to business processes to outputs to outcomes, may be a useful way of measuring the impact of KM in organizations.
- A measurement system actually works.

Keeping up with competition certainly is in the minds of senior executives. If one consulting firm is applying knowledge management systems more effectively than another consulting firm, resulting in more bids awarded to the former consulting firm, then this may trigger the need to more fully leverage the knowledge management systems in the latter consulting firm. If one pharmaceutical company is greatly reducing its drug discovery process and time to market partly through using an in-house knowledge management system, then this may cause concern by other pharmaceutical companies. In today's environment, organizations need to be adaptive and agile and must, as the saying goes, "work smarter, not harder." Knowledge management is a way to help achieve this goal to produce the outcomes necessary for a company's future viability.

OUTCOME MEASURES

The aforementioned APQC "Measuring the Impact of Knowledge Management" study (www.apqc.org) found that organizations generally do not create separate KM measures of outcomes. Rather, they apply the business measures of outcomes and then work backward to design KM measures and activities to concentrate on those outcomes. Outcome measures may relate to revenues or profits, or to customer satisfaction and loyalty. These would be contrasted with output measures, such as productivity or goods/services produced.

An outcome measure is usually associated with strategic effectiveness and long-term success. An outcome measure may look at whether the KM effort has reduced the risk of doing business. Or perhaps it has increased employee loyalty or customer satisfaction. In the university setting, learning outcomes are typically included in a course syllabus. These learning outcomes will hopefully provide ways for the student to "learn how to learn" in order to engage in continuous learning for the long term.

SUMMARY

We have explored some issues and simple measures that could be used to assess the value of knowledge management efforts to whet one's appetite. In the next chapter, we will examine valuation approaches for KM in more depth.

REFERENCES

Alber, J. 2004. "Rethinking ROI: Managing Risk and Rewards in KM Initiatives." Available from www.llrx.com/features/rethinkingroi.htm (February 23).

Anderson, M. 2002. "Measuring Intangible Value: The ROI of Knowledge Management." American Society for Training and Development. Available from www1.astd.org/news_letter/November/Links/anderson.html (November).

APQC. n.d. "Measuring the Impact of Knowledge Management." Available from www.apqc.org.

Bontis, N. 2002. *World Congress of Intellectual Capital Readings*. Boston: Elsevier Butterworth-Heinemann/KMCI Press.

Brooking, A. 1996. *Intellectual Capital: Core Assets for the Third Millennium Enterprise*. London: International Thomson Business Press.

Edvinsson, L., and M. Malone. 1997. *Intellectual Capital*. Cambridge, MA: Harvard Business Press.

Flamholtz, E. 2003. "Putting Balance and Validity into the Balanced Scorecard," *Journal of Human Resource Costing and Accounting* 17 (3).

Gold, A., A. Malhotra, and A. Segars. 2001. "Knowledge Management: An Organizational Capabilities Perspective," *Journal of Management Information Systems* 18 (1).

Housel, T., and A. Bell. 2001. *Measuring and Managing Knowledge*. New York: McGraw Hill/Irwin.

Jacoby, G., and Luqi. 2007. "Intranet Model and Metrics," *Communications of the ACM* 50 (2).

Kankanhalli, A., and B. Tan. 2004. "A Review of Metrics for Knowledge Management Systems and Knowledge Management Initiatives." Proceedings of the 37th Hawaii International Conference for System Sciences, IEEE.

Kay, S. 2003. "Cost, Value, and ROI for Knowledge Management in Law Firms." Available from www.llrx.com/features/kmcost.htm (August 31).

Knowledge@Wharton. 2001. "Measuring Returns on IT Investments: Some Tools and Techniques." The Wharton School, University of Pennsylvania. Available from http://knowledge.wharton.upenn.edu (July 18).

Lev, B. 2001. *Intangibles: Management, Measurement, and Reporting*. Washington, DC: Brookings Institution Press.

Liebowitz, J. 2005. "Developing Metrics for Determining Knowledge Management Success: A Fuzzy Logic Approach," *Issues in Information Systems* 6 (2).

Liebowitz, J., and C. Suen. 2000. "Developing Knowledge Management Metrics for Measuring Intellectual Capital," *Journal of Intellectual Capital* 1 (1).

Liebowitz, J., and K. Wright. 1999. "Does Measuring Knowledge Make 'Cents'?" *Expert Systems With Applications: An International Journal* 17.

Martin, K. 2002. "Show Me the Money: Measuring the Return on Knowledge Management." Available from www.llrx.com/features/kmroi.htm. (October 15).

National Electronic Library for Health. 2005. "Prove It: Measuring the Value of Knowledge Management." Available from www.nelh.nhs.uk/knowledge_management/km2/measurement.asp.

Roos, J., G. Roos, L. Edvinsson, and N. Dragonetti. 1998. *Intellectual Capital*. London: Palgrave Macmillan Business.

Smith, H., and J. McKeen. 2004. "Marketing KM to the Organization, CAIS, www.aisnet.org.

Sveiby, K. E. 1997. *The New Organizational Wealth: Managing and Measuring Knowledge-Based Assets.* San Francisco: Berrett-Koehler Publishers.

Tobin, T. 2004. "The Insider's Guide to Knowledge Management ROI." White paper, ServiceWare Technologies/Knova (February).

Wickhorst, V. 2002. "Measuring the ROI on Knowledge Management Systems." *Performance Improvement Quarterly* 15 (2).

4

Thoughts on Measuring Successful Knowledge Management Practices

Jay Liebowitz

Senior management typically is interested in knowing the "value" of their knowledge management (KM) efforts. The old adage, "If we can't measure it, we can't manage it," seems to surface in conversations with senior leaders in organizations. Knowledge management is no different.

However, the knowledge management community still needs to put more rigor into measuring the value of the knowledge management efforts in order to instill more science to complement the art of KM. Elsa Rhoads, the knowledge and performance architect at the Pension Benefit Guaranty Corporation, shared some of her survey results at the Braintrust International 2007 Conference. She surveyed the Knowledge Management Working Group of the Federal Chief Information Officer's (CIO) Council. The respondents included 125 individual participants from twenty-six federal organizations with a 38 percent overall response rate. When asked, "How do agencies measure successful KM practices?" the survey population indicated that 23 percent of the agencies had no formal measurement system, and 13 percent don't standardize measurement. Additional leading responses from this question were: 16 percent used employee surveys; 10 percent balanced scorecard; 9 percent benchmarking; 8 percent anecdotal stories; 6 percent metrics for ROI; 5 percent Baldrige criteria.

In APQC's benchmarking study on "Measuring the Impact of Knowledge Management" (2003), the partner organizations in the study were able to double their return on their knowledge management investments. APQC (n.d.) keeps a set of standard performance measures as related to the knowledge management functions and processes. These measures, which are kept as part of APQC's KM database, are:

Cost

- Total cost of communities of practice per revenue
- Total cost of best practice transfer processes per revenue
- Total cost of after-action reviews per revenue
- Total cost of lessons learned processed per revenue
- Total cost of expertise locator systems per revenue
- Total cost of content management systems per revenue
- Total cost of virtual collaboration per revenue
- Total cost of knowledge management per revenue
- Percentage of participation costs per total cost
- Percentage of travel and meeting costs per total cost
- Percentage of financial impact that is cost savings
- Percentage of financial impact that is revenue gain
- Percentage of financial impact that is quality improvement
- Percentage of financial impact that is cost avoidance
- Percentage of financial impact that is productivity increase

Process Efficiency

- Number of full-time equivalents for the KM program per revenue
- Percentage of management emphasis on qualitative indicators and measures of improvement
- Percentage of management emphasis on quantitative measures of knowledge management program expansion and participation
- Percentage of knowledge-sharing/reuse objectives
- Percentage of communities of practice under way as a part of knowledge management
- Percentage of best practice transfer process under way as a part of knowledge management
- Percentage of after-action reviews under way as a part of knowledge management
- Percentage of lessons learned process under way as a part of knowledge management
- Percentage of expertise locator systems under way as a part of knowledge management
- Percentage of content management systems under way as a part of knowledge management
- Percentage of virtual collaboration under way as a part of knowledge management

- Percentage of knowledge retention under way as a part of knowledge management
- Number of formal communities of practice
- Total number of community participants
- Number of informal communities of practice
- Total number of informal participants
- Percentage of financial impact attributed to communities of practice
- Percentage of communities of practice that have developed metrics
- Percentage of communities of practice with metrics
- Percentage of formal communities of practice with metrics
- Percentage of informal communities of practice with metrics

Companies are experiencing wide usage of their knowledge management initiatives. For example, Unisys cites the following, per the Braintrust International 2007 conference:

- 36,000 SharePoint users worldwide
- 100 percent services employees with KM performance objectives
- 11,600 employee "my sites" in use
- 1,067 client collaboration team rooms
- 70+ officially chartered knowledge communities
- 183 sales executives use SharePoint to track opportunities. (Institute for International Research n.d.)

With these types of numbers, worker and team productivity should increase, as well as the possible generation of new ideas through the various collaboration sites.

Buckman Labs, a manufacturer of specialty chemicals, is another company that has been a leader in the knowledge management field. They have a website called Knowledge Nurture (www.knowledge-nurture.com) to help Buckman Labs employees learn about knowledge management. They also were one of the pioneers to emphasize the need and use of a knowledge network, called K'netix. An interview with Mike Anderson, the director of information systems at Buckman Labs, gives some insight:

> Buckman's knowledge network will also become more robust. From Anderson's vantage point, it is difficult to put a dollar figure on the value of this resource. However, the overall benefit is clear for everyone to see. "K'netix is fundamental to the way we do business, so reporting and ETL figure prominently in everything we do," Anderson concludes. "By focusing on one integrated set of tools for reporting, analysis, and data integration, I believe we will have a much more efficient environment two or three years from now than we do today. That's where the ROI comes from—by focusing on a

single, capable solution, then leveraging that expertise throughout the organization." (Information Builders n.d.)

Geisler (2007) points out various impacts and benefits of knowledge management to users and beneficiaries of knowledge in organizations. Some of these include:

- Improved level of education and literacy
- Improved individual competence
- Improved level of motivation and satisfaction
- Improved sense of empowerment
- Improved communications, relationships, and use of the KM system
- Improved efficiency of operations
- Increased productivity
- Improved growth and market share
- Reduced barriers to innovation and trade
- Improved rates of ideas generated
- Improved competitiveness
- Higher rate of dissemination of knowledge

Related to the benefits of knowledge management is the concept of how recognition and rewards come into play to encourage knowledge-sharing activities. Extrinsic motivators typically deal with rewards and are temporary in nature. Intrinsic motivators favor recognition and altruism and are typically more permanent than extrinsic motivators. Some recent research by Lee and Ahn (2007) demonstrates that group-based reward is less efficient than individual-based reward. However, most organizations will use both individual and group-based rewards and recognition. The basic foundation is to build a firm level of interpersonal trust so that people will be encouraged to share what they know. Two major types of trust are competence-based trust and benevolence-based trust. Competence-based trust is that you seek knowledge from an individual due to his/her respected expertise and competence. Benevolence-based trust is that one is willing to share his/her knowledge for the good of the organization and the feeling that given another set of conditions, the other person would be likely to reciprocate. Knowledge is typically shared dependent upon the value of the knowledge that is conveyed and reciprocity.

Knowledge management should be tied to deriving business value. According to Williams and Williams (2007), "in economic terms, the business value of an investment (asset) is the net present value of the after-tax cash flows associated with the investment." In terms of business intelligence, for example, Williams and Williams believe that delivering business value via business intelligence should either improve management processes so that management can increase revenues, reduce costs, or both, or improve operational processes so that the business can increase revenues, reduce costs, or both. Similarly, knowledge management should also derive business value through improving management or operational processes; however, these may be harder to define than through using business intelligence software. Knowledge management could provide savings and improvement in organizational quality and efficiency or reduce the time to find relevant information and people, but could be difficult to measure in terms of the organization adapting quickly to unanticipated changes through using KM initiatives. On the brighter side, though, KM can be measured in terms of increasing the sense of belonging and trust among employees (through using an employee culture survey), improving communication and coordination across the organization, and increasing customer satisfaction. A key criterion in assessing KM efforts is to develop the value proposition. There should be an explicit alignment between the KM strategy and the organization's business strategy.

MEASURING KNOWLEDGE FLOWS

If knowledge causes action to take place, then the flows of knowledge could be measured by the knowledge-based actions that are applied. Here is an example. Let's assume we have a project manager with a team of four individuals. Each of these individuals has a specific type of subject matter domain expertise that contributes to the team. The project manager has a general background. One team member is a nuclear physicist, another is a chemist, another has a business background, and the last has an information technology background. The goal of their team is to develop an integrated course dealing with analytical methods for their entry-level employees to take as part of their overall orientation program.

The team first determines the expected learning objectives and learning outcomes for the course. Then, they determine the knowledge units that they feel should be taught as part of the course. The next step is to package the knowledge units in such a way that they encourage the student to be an integrated problem solver in science and technology. Modules are then developed using these packaged knowledge units and various teaching techniques are introduced to best convey the material in these modules. An issues-based approach might be used where there is an oil spill, and various chemical, environmental, and business concerns are introduced as part of this issue on how to best clean up the oil spill.

In this project team, various knowledge flows exist between the different team members. There is subject matter domain knowledge, operational knowledge, coordination knowledge, process knowledge, and perhaps strategic knowledge that may be passed between each team member, as well as between the students who will learn these modules. For the students, they can make decisions based on the analytical techniques they apply from the knowledge they acquire relating to the context of the issue or problem. These knowledge-based actions can be correct or not, depending upon the particular case at hand. For the project team members, their knowledge-based actions can be determined based upon the activities generated from the team members and whether the team's knowledge-based actions have a positive or negative impact on tangibles or intangibles.

CONVINCING MANAGEMENT OF KM'S WORTH IN TERMS OF KNOWLEDGE RETENTION

Knowledge management may seem amorphous to senior management, due to its seemingly "touchy-feely" aspect. Of course, management is interested in "the bottom line" and how KM can contribute to the organization's strategic mission. One way to help convince management is to discuss KM in terms of "lost" knowledge opportunities. Many organizations are embarking on knowledge retention efforts in order to capture the experiential learning of experts before they retire or leave the organization. These knowledge retention programs contribute directly to workforce development and succession planning—which have direct impacts on an organization's productivity.

In one part of a major government organization, about one-third of its senior executives are eligible to retire within the next three years. They have recognized the difficulties they may have in terms of institutional knowledge loss and individualized expertise loss when these individuals retire. To address this concern, the organization has embarked on a knowledge retention and succession planning effort to ensure that these key learnings and critical knowledge don't walk out the door. The high-level knowledge retention strategy being considered is:

1. Determine attrition profiles
2. Determine the organization's workforce of the future
3. Develop competencies
4. Develop migration paths
5. Create the organization's university and on-the-job training programs to fill knowledge gaps and promote succession planning
6. Develop performance management structure
7. Apply knowledge management recommendations for workforce development, community building, and knowledge retention.

Another organization, as part of developing its Strategic Human Capital Plan, has included a "Leadership and Knowledge Retention" pillar as part of the overall human capital strategy. In the part related to knowledge retention, the focus has been identified as: Implement a knowledge-retention and knowledge-sharing program, leveraging expertise of current employees to meet current and future mission requirements. To achieve this knowledge-retention and knowledge-sharing focus, three goals are cited: (1) identify knowledge-retention needs in order to leverage expertise of current employees to meet mission requirements, (2) create an inventory of current knowledge-retention strengths and deficits, and (3) establish knowledge-sharing practices, processes, and systems in order to leverage knowledge internally and externally.

Senior management can appreciate the potential impact of a "brain drain" effect on the organization through retirement or attrition. After all, they themselves are usually part of that knowledge loss that may be happening shortly as they retire. Thus, it isn't very difficult to get them to visualize the potential impact on the organization, whether from the loss of their informal networks that they have established with customers, employees, and clients or resulting from the loss of their own technical expertise or historical institutional knowledge that they possess. Capturing and sharing the critical at-risk knowledge that is strategic to the organization's mission is an important component for developing the knowledge base of the organization for future success.

SHORT CASE STUDY: FRONT-END
KNOWLEDGE-BASED VISA INTERACTIVE ADVISOR

As part of an effort to perform knowledge retention and capture business rules to help the general public navigate through the murky visa process waters, a front-end knowledge-based visa interactive advisor could help guide the general public through the rules and regulations relating to PERM, H1B, H2A, and H2B visas. One way to better inform the user is through a knowledge-based interactive advisor. This would be similar to the rule-based expert system advisors, called ELAWS, which the U.S. Department of Labor (DOL) already has been using over recent years.

ELAWS stands for Employment Laws Assistance for Workers and Small Businesses. Currently, there are about twenty-five ELAWS advisors at the DOL's ELAWS website (www.dol.gov/elaws). These include:

- Drug-Free Workplace Advisor
- Family & Medical Leave Act (FMLA) Advisor
- Federal Contractor Compliance Advisor

- FirstStep Employment Law Advisor
- Fair Labor Standards Act (FLSA) Advisor
- FLSA Coverage & Employment Status Advisor
- FLSA Overtime Security Advisor
- FLSA Hours Worked Advisor
- FLSA Child Labor Rules Advisor
- FLSA Section 14 (c) Advisor (Special Minimum Wage)
- Health Benefits Advisor
- MSHA Online Forms Advisor
- MSHA Training Plan Advisor
- MSHA Fire Suppression & Fire Protection Advisor
- OSHA Confined Spaces Advisor
- OSHA Fire Safety Advisor
- OSHA Hazard Awareness Advisor
- OSHA Lead in Construction Advisor
- OSHA Software Expert Advisors
- Poster Advisor
- REALifelines Advisor
- Small Business Retirement Savings Advisor
- Uniformed Services Employment & Reemployment Rights Act (USERRA) Advisor
- Veterans' Preference Advisor
- e-VETS Resource Advisor

These ELAWS advisors could be used either over the Web in an interactive user session, or downloaded as executables for use on one's computer. They were created with the expert system shell, CORVID, by Exsys, Inc. According to Exsys, more than 40,000 advisors have been downloaded from Occupational Safety and Health Administration (OSHA's) websites per year, resulting in over $100 million per year savings for businesses in terms of consulting and legal fees (Exsys n.d.). The United States Department of Agriculture (USDA) and Small Business Administration (SBA) have also used Exsys' CORVID for their work as well.

The visa interactive advisor could be built using Exsys's CORVID. The typical process to follow is to perform problem selection, knowledge acquisition, knowledge representation, knowledge encoding, knowledge testing and evaluation, and implementation and maintenance. These knowledge engineering steps are accomplished iteratively, in terms of applying rapid prototyping as the system development lifecycle approach. The problem selection stage would involve segmenting the potential knowledge base into PERM, H1B, H2A, and H2B visa components. Knowledge acquisition would then consist of interviewing multiple experts in these respective areas, as well as reviewing existing documentation. Knowledge representation would be the next stage whereby the knowledge is developed into the rule-based format, and knowledge encoding would convert these rules into Exsys's CORVID expert system shell. Knowledge testing and evaluation would involve running hard, soft, and special subcases against the knowledge base to check for completeness, consistency, and accuracy. Typically, the knowledge base will need to be refined and the iterative steps of knowledge acquisition, knowledge representation, knowledge encoding, and knowledge testing would commence again. Once some desired level of accuracy is obtained, user evaluation of the system would also be conducted and user recommendations for improvements would be considered and incorporated as appropriate. Of course, the information in the knowledge base would need to be vetted through the U.S. Department of Labor, especially through Legal.

The advantages of a visa interactive advisor are many: improved information flow to users; improved response times to needed information; enhanced public image of DOL in terms of using the state-of-the-art types of systems; increased efficiency and effectiveness on the part of DOL, as employees are able to free up their time to answer the more difficult, versus routine, user questions. The main drawback of this approach is that an operations and maintenance team would need to be established to update the visa interactive advisor if laws change. In the experience of the ELAWS advisors, the advantages have greatly outweighed any disadvantages and a very positive experience has resulted on the part of the general public and DOL. In fact, the ELAWS effort has received numerous government awards in the past.

SUMMARY

Showing value from knowledge management efforts is expected by management. How that value is derived can be a challenging process. This chapter and the previous ones provided some insight on ways to show benefits from KM, whether through hard metrics or through anecdotal evidence. The forthcoming chapters in the second part of this book are actual cases of real KM projects that will also explain how they derived value from their KM efforts.

REFERENCES

APQC. 2003. "Measuring the Impact of Knowledge Management." Available from www.apqc.org.
APQC. n.d. "The Open Standards Benchmarking Collaborative Database: Knowledge Management." Available from www.apqc.org/PDF/osbc/km/measures.pdf.

Exsys. n.d. Available from www.exsys.com.

Geisler, E. 2007. "A Typology of Knowledge Management: Strategic Groups and Role Behavior in Organizations," *Journal of Knowledge Management* 11 (1).

Information Builders. n.d. "Buckman Labs Improves Knowledge Management With WebFOCUS" Available from www.informationbuilders.com/applications/buckman.html.

Institute for International Research. n.d. Available from www.iirusa.com.

Lee, D. J., and J. H. Ahn. 2007. "Reward Systems for Intra-Organizational Knowledge Sharing," *European Journal of Operational Research* 180.

Williams, S., and N. Williams. 2007. *The Profit Impact of Business Intelligence*. Boston: Morgan Kaufmann Publishers/Elsevier.

II

CASE STUDIES

5

Knowledge Management and Organizational Learning at the Annie E. Casey Foundation

Helping Disadvantaged Kids and Families

Thomas E. Kern

The Annie E. Casey Foundation has been working to promote the well-being of vulnerable children and families for nearly sixty years. Established in 1948 by UPS cofounder Jim Casey and his siblings to honor their mother, the Foundation's first grants supported a camp for disadvantaged children near the Casey family home in Seattle. Later, Jim Casey steered the Foundation's efforts toward finding more stable placements for children being bounced from one foster family to another.

In the 1980s, the Foundation shifted its focus toward improving the effectiveness of public systems—from education to child welfare to juvenile justice—that too often undermine families' strengths and create dependency. Today, the Foundation supports a diverse range of activities with a mission to build better futures for millions of American children at risk of poor educational, economic, social, and health outcomes. Its work is divided into three main areas: reforming public systems, promoting accountability and innovation, and transforming tough neighborhoods into family supporting communities.

Headquartered in Baltimore, with a direct services component providing foster care and family services throughout New England, the Foundation makes grants that help states, cities, and neighborhoods fashion more creative, cost-effective responses to the challenges facing children and families whose circumstances place them at risk of not succeeding.

KNOWLEDGE MANAGEMENT AND ORGANIZATIONAL LEARNING: ITS ORIGINS AT CASEY

The Foundation's long-standing commitment to helping disadvantaged kids, families, and the neighborhoods in which they live benefited significantly from an increase in its endowment in the late 1990s. Newly available resources were directed to (1) fund a larger staff, (2) make more encompassing investments to develop comprehensive and integrated social strategies in a number of urban centers, and (3) establish a strategic consulting arm to help advise states and localities on ways to improve their public-service systems to work better for children, families, and communities. This growth in staffing and investments, along with the increasing complexity of the Foundation's work, posed challenges to its ability to take full advantage of the wealth of information and knowledge its efforts were generating. In response, the Foundation's senior leadership authorized a study (first an internal one in 2001, and then as the magnitude of the challenge became better known, a 2002 study drawing on external consulting support) of current knowledge management (KM) practices at the Foundation and how well they supported its mission to help disadvantaged kids and their families.

The study began by identifying the obstacles to knowledge sharing that were impeding staff from breaking out of their program silos. An analysis and detailed staff survey brought several issues to the forefront. First, accessing the most current and relevant knowledge across all programs was hindered by the lack of a centralized system for finding information. Second, staff members' heavy workloads meant that they had limited time to spend publicizing new knowledge—especially when there was no structured way for doing this. Third, Casey's organizational culture made overreliance on informal (and therefore potentially less comprehensive) networks for exchanging knowledge the norm. Exemplified by its growing community work (see text box 5.1), all of this was happening in an environment in which there were increasing demands on staff to have wider knowledge about related programs in addition to their own specialist skills. This was coupled with the understanding that if Casey was not sharing its expertise adequately with its own staff, it was likely not doing much better to leverage these resources with grantees, stakeholders, policymakers, and other foundations.

Simply put, the 2002 study suggested that a large part of the valuable knowledge that Foundation initiatives were developing was not easily and readily obtainable and useful by staff, consultants, grantees, and colleague organizations, thereby undercutting Casey's efforts to achieve its mission. In some respects, the assessment amounted to a kind of "business intelli-

---

TEXT BOX 5.1. KNOWLEDGE MANAGEMENT AT AECF

In 1999, the Casey Foundation concentrated some of its grants to launch *Making Connections*, an initiative to develop comprehensive and integrated social strategies in a few impoverished urban centers. The transformation meant that Casey had to hire new staff to support the expanded work. In addition, the role of its program officers, known as senior associates, changed: from being national, single-issue experts on subjects such as child welfare and juvenile justice, several became generalists leading cross-functional teams in one or two cities. Two problems, both relating to knowledge challenges, emerged as a result of these organizational moves. First, since the cross-functional approach meant that senior associates were now working in areas beyond their expertise, they needed more information from colleagues to do their work successfully. Moreover, many new staff members had a limited understanding of the history of the Foundation or the best practice it had learned over time. More often than not, they could get this information only by asking their longer-serving colleagues for it. What they needed to know wasn't written down; it had remained in people's heads. Second, what knowledge management there had been at the Foundation was in danger of diminishing. With the experts' time fragmented, no one took responsibility for managing the organization's knowledge in any single area. Meanwhile, senior associates, already busy in their cross-functional roles, were too distracted by requests for information from colleagues to begin generating and applying new knowledge to their grant-making and policy work.

From "Knowledge Management Comes to Philanthropy" by Marla M. Capozzi, Stephanie M. Lowell, and Les Silverman, *McKinsey Quarterly*, 2003 Special Edition.

---

gence" gathering for the Foundation. As a nonprofit organization, foundations need this tool as much as businesses do to assess organizational performance against a set of measures that inform them of their effectiveness in achieving the outcomes they seek. The study also included a "competitive intelligence" component in which the practices of comparable organizations were benchmarked, affirming that most foundations face the same challenges and identifying some model practices for the Casey Foundation to consider for its own use.

A STATEMENT OF PURPOSE,
CORE ELEMENTS, AND INITIAL PRIORITIES

The Casey Foundation's leadership believed that critical to Casey's ability to address the needs of disadvantaged kids and their families and neighborhoods is an understanding of (1) what works, (2) what it has learned in the past, and (3) how everyone can learn from each other, both within the Foundation and through partnerships with others. The 2002 study helped increase the Foundation's clarity around these challenges and with the study's findings and recommendations in hand, senior leadership created a new department—Knowledge Services—locating it within the Foundation's strategic consulting group to implement the study's recommendations. The Foundation hired a senior associate to assume overall responsibility and manage Knowledge Services' daily operations, which was built on the preexisting library unit now to be transformed to address a range of knowledge management and organizational learning activities. Knowledge Services worked with several key departments—information technology, evaluation, and communications—to draw on their expertise to implement a knowledge management strategy.

Supported by the 2002 study's findings and senior leadership input, the new Knowledge Services team identified the purpose of knowledge management and organizational learning at Casey to

> Improve access to Foundation knowledge, promote better understanding of the nuance and scope of what it has learned, and where possible, facilitate the effective creation and leveraging of relevant knowledge to better achieve its outcomes by addressing the information needs of its key audiences (including practitioners, policymakers, researchers, the media, and other funders and non-profits working in areas similar to Casey's).

In practical terms, the Foundation realized that knowledge management should focus on ways to better create, organize, share, and apply the knowledge it needs for its work. It began with six key elements to help guide its efforts. These had come out of the 2002 study.

1) Develop an organized knowledge architecture for staff to access knowledge across multiple program areas while creating new knowledge relevant and organized for users. Benefits would include the ability of staff to more easily and rapidly browse for the knowledge they need, greater consistency in the formats for knowledge creation, and clarity around how the Foundation might wish to direct its investments in knowledge development and cross-cutting activities.

2) Leverage technology to support KM to help improve knowledge creation and sharing by centralizing these activities for knowledge creators and improving their distribution for users. If accomplished, this could provide authors with one central location to input knowledge into their taxonomies, maintain a single place to look with knowledge requests, and offer centralized administration of the systems to ensure continuous upgrading based on user needs and available technology.

3) Establish robust KM processes to ensure systematic implementation across the Foundation. Key benefits to this work are the assurance that all knowledge areas are organized consistently; that gaps in knowledge, if they exist, can be more readily identified and acted upon; and that routine procedures will ensure new resources are collected regularly to maintain currency.

4) Clarify KM roles in the Foundation to allow it to organize and implement KM successfully against specified goals. Benefits here are focus for the work and reduction of redundancy, a helpful delineation of expectations and responsibilities, and the dedication of full-time resources to a central function that can ensure experts throughout the Foundation have effective support.

5) Foster a learning and teaching culture to ensure a strong organizational basis to support and encourage ongoing KM initiatives. Learning programs and curriculum can help facilitate knowledge sharing, supported by job descriptions and performance standards and evaluations that emphasize their value and importance.

6) Set strategic KM objectives supported by leadership to help ensure senior management focus and alignment with the Foundation's mission. If staff understands senior leadership's support for the work and its alignment with Foundation priorities, theirs will match it.

These elements would eventually infuse much of Casey's knowledge tools and services development.

The 2002 study recommended a number of specific actions, primary among them the creation of a flagship, Web-based knowledge management system for Casey staff, consultants, and grantees. Equally important, although less resource and time intensive, was the call to integrate the Foundation's library services with KM, provide support to help staff in their knowledge development and documentation efforts, develop a range of tools to improve awareness and integration of Casey programs, and be attentive to the longer-term challenge of supporting the Foundation's efforts as a learning organization.

With a new department, a statement of purpose, a set of guiding core elements, and initial priorities in place, the Foundation officially began its knowledge management implementation in early 2003.

ASSESSING KNOWLEDGE MANAGEMENT'S EFFECTIVENESS SO FAR: FIVE VALUATION APPROACHES

The emergent literature in knowledge management speaks to the importance of being able to measure the impact of KM in the organization as an essential element in refining its efforts and justifying its expense. Effective measurement depends on at least two things: agreement on the outcomes being sought after and workable measures that can help identify what difference the KM initiative is making to achieve those outcomes.

For the Casey Foundation, its commitment to improving the lives of disadvantaged kids, their families, and the neighborhoods in which they live is central to all of its work. An initiative like KM must provide direct support to the grant and service programs with these goals in mind. Although these broadly framed outcomes make it difficult to differentiate the impact that individual (and, in particular, supporting or cross-cutting) departments have, they nonetheless crystallize everyone's efforts and offer the basis for detailed and measurable indicators and performance measures around each grant investment strategy. A helpful mantra of the Foundation's results-based accountability initiative calls on all departments to design their programs with a threefold evaluation framework in mind: What did we do? How well did we do it? Is anyone better off? This way of thinking invites both a qualitative and a quantitative assessment of the work that looks at outputs (how many products were generated) and outcomes (how many kids, families, and neighborhoods were positively affected). Coupled with the six key elements of the KM initiative listed earlier, the performance management framework gives the Foundation a way to assess knowledge management and build on its efforts.

To help with the measurement conversation, another factor to include is cost. Although information on the actual cost of planning, start-up, and implementation of KM at the Foundation is proprietary, it can be said that the costs in question primarily include staff and consultant time and the cost of information technology hardware and software. The costs focused on the following tasks:

- An outside consultant engagement to (1) assess the status of knowledge use and sharing at the Foundation, (2) pilot several KM approaches for review by management, and (3) recommend a KM strategy for the Foundation to consider.
- Establishment and maintenance of a Knowledge Services unit, consolidated with the Foundation's library. Services provided by this unit would included designing and populating the Foundation's internal KM System; provision of online tools and research services to support program staff; promoting and sharing the Foundation's knowledge assets within and outside Casey; and support to help develop and capture knowledge resources, as requested.
- Requirements analysis and selection of a hardware/software solutions to contain the Foundation's proposed internal KM System.

- Collateral staff time from other departments, including the Information Technology, Communications, and program departments to help design services and identify and submit content.

With these considerations in mind, several different valuation methods have influenced the Foundation's view and application of Knowledge Management. They are:

- Valuing the Foundation's knowledge assets to weigh the extent of Casey's investment in knowledge management
- Factoring in the knowledge management life cycle to keep the timing of KM's impact in perspective
- Using the return on investment (ROI) metric as a reality check on Foundation KM expenditures
- Applying the balanced scorecard to ensure investments and impacts are kept in equilibrium
- Taking the pulse of the organizational culture: How do staff think and act relative to the Foundation's most important asset—its knowledge?

The idea of using several approaches rather than one is influenced greatly by the challenge that nonprofits face relative to for-profit institutions. In the case of for-profits, costs are tracked in terms of profit centers with a specific result or bottom line in mind from which a return on investment can be clearly calculated and assessed. Not only are cost centers not usually applied in nonprofits, the assessment of nonprofit performance is further complicated by the more difficult to measure outcomes to which an organization like Casey is committed.

KM AT CASEY: AN ASSESSMENT OF ITS FIRST YEARS

Casey's six key KM elements call on the Foundation to:

1) Develop an organized knowledge architecture.
2) Leverage technology to help improve knowledge creation and sharing.
3) Establish robust KM processes.
4) Clarify KM roles in the Foundation.
5) Foster a learning and teaching culture.
6) Set strategic KM objectives supported by leadership.

With these in mind, here is an assessment of Casey's KM efforts so far.

Valuing the Foundation's Knowledge Assets to Weigh
the Extent of Casey's Investment in Knowledge Management

The philanthropic sector is often assessed in terms of the size of the financial assets in charitable foundations. The top fifteen foundations each have assets ranging from $3 billion to more than $30 billion. By any standard, that is a lot of money. However, more current thinking suggests that the real value of a foundation is not so much its endowment or annual grant-making portfolio, but rather the knowledge assets its financial investments have created. These intangible assets are sometimes defined as the organization's (1) *intellectual capital or human capital* (the knowledge and skills of people that can only ever be partially spun off into discrete products that become part of a larger public domain); (2) *relationship or networking capital* (the knowledge resident in the social system in which the organization is invested and engaged); and (3) *structural capital* (the knowledge embedded in the organization and its ability to draw on its human capital to network and create impact, influence, and leverage in the fields to which it is committed).

With this in mind, Casey's knowledge management efforts in the first three and a half years of the initiative has helped stimulate Foundation conversation around Casey's knowledge assets or resources. KM's central tenets—providing tools and approaches to help create, organize, share, and apply knowledge—focus on Casey's intangible assets of knowledge and learning, all with the purpose of helping kids and families. A look at these six elements shows progress has been made in each. A knowledge roadmap serves as the organizing principle for its mature, developing, and cross-cutting work. Technology is in place and periodically enhanced to provide a means for organizing and sharing these resources. Staff is routinely challenged to contribute resources they develop or fund and to think harder about creating them with key users in mind as part of their job. And the Foundation's leadership has likewise called on the staff to

---

TEXT BOX 5.2.
AN ORGANIZATION'S KNOWLEDGE ASSETS

Three Key Elements

Intellectual or Human Capital (the knowledge and skills of its people)
Relationship or Networking Capital (the knowledge resident in the systems in which the organization is engaged)
Structural Capital (the knowledge in the organization and its ability to draw on human capital)

find and use the time and space they need to do better at knowledge creation and application, all with intent to have the greatest impact, influence, and leverage in their work.

Factoring in the Knowledge Management Life Cycle to Keep the Timing of KM's Impact in Perspective

Knowledge management is a relatively new field, drawing from earlier thinking around quality assurance/quality control and Total Quality Management, among others. Like other cross-cutting management initiatives, KM involves a gestation period in which strategic design and implementation take time, particularly as approaches become embedded in the organizational culture and as they seek to support and have an impact in a number of diverse programs. The American Productivity and Quality Center's *Road Map to Knowledge Management Results* (O'Dell 2000) identifies several stages of implementation, each of which require an involvement of time, money, and staff commitment to be successful. The stages (getting started, developing a strategy, designing and launching a KM initiative, expanding and supporting it, and institutionalizing KM) offer a useful barometer for an organization to see where it is and modulate its expectations and assessment.

Casey's three-and-one-half-year initiative places it in between stages four and five: expanding and supporting KM and institutionalizing it throughout the organization. Spearheaded by early visionary thinking by a key senior leader, Casey intensively assessed its situation (via a KM audit) and developed a comprehensive strategy, backed up by sufficient financial resources and staffing to pilot and then more formally implement a KM framework. Since then, senior leadership has periodically circled back to support KM's role at the Foundation by endorsing the creation of new services (like a public KM System accessible through a revamped Foundation

---

TEXT BOX 5.3.
KNOWLEDGE MANAGEMENT LIFE CYCLE

Five Key Stages

Getting Started
Developing a Strategy
Designing and Launching a KM Initiative
Expanding and Supporting It
Institutionalizing KM

website), building job descriptions for all staff to ensure everyone's knowledge management role is clear, and fostering dialogue around more effective, user-oriented product development. What remains for Casey is what is at the heart of any institutionalization phase worth its salt—the need for persistent application, learning, and adaptation as a consequence of Casey's knowledge creation such that it becomes a seamless part of its culture and ethic. This takes time and this is what the KM life cycle is all about.

Using the Return on Investment Metric as a
Reality Check on Foundation KM Expenditures

At the heart of a return on investment (ROI) approach is the question: What benefits did we get to justify the costs we incurred? Implicit to the question is the belief (or hope) that costs and benefits can be accurately and completely measured. Without a full picture, the conclusion can be imbalanced, misleading, and damaging to the organization's resource allocation and program impact. Yet many of the costs and benefits belie accurate measure, making it difficult to rely on ROI alone to assess progress.

For Casey, a look at the ROI for its KM initiative entails three sets of costing challenges. First, Casey quantified the costs identified in the previous section regarding direct staff time and IT-related expenditures. These were the easiest costs to quantify. A second, harder set of costing challenges related to the opportunity costs of staffers who spent collateral time on this work as opposed to what they might have done had they not been asked to liaise with or undertake tasks for KM. This kind of measurement is problematic, but one way to get at it is to identify the kinds of tasks that comprise the work depending on what professional level of the staff person, multiplied by the number of staff involved. Casey did not try to cost this in dollars, but does emphasize the value of these shared or collaborative efforts and endorses the time and effort needed to make them happen.

The third and most challenging cost exercise had to do with pricing the benefits. One benefit is time savings due to more efficiently compiled and organized knowledge resources that enabled staff to respond faster and better to inquiries, resulting in efficiencies in forwarding needed materials or forgoing conversations because written materials were available that could answer questions. Another benefit is the improved chance that the most relevant resources are identified and directed to users, improving their ability to address their needs. After all, while savings related to process and work flow is important, the real ROI is when knowledge is used to successfully help a child or family. How does one calculate that value?

On the other hand, the availability of greater resources might lead to more time spent than otherwise by experts to review and adapt materials to their work. Is this a cost or benefit? If the assumption is that the knowledge resources helped contribute to better decision making, then this benefit would show up in leading to better program outcomes. And if you could identify all these incidents of better knowledge sharing, faster learning, and better decision making, what is the dollar value you place on it?

For Casey, the fact that these considerations are now a part of its dialogue has helped elevate the importance of KM tools and approaches within and across programs. Several years into the initiative, programs are focused more than ever on tailoring knowledge to address user needs and building learning agendas and communities to foster dialogue and application. As these approaches evolve, metrics around them will likely form and help assess their effectiveness.

Applying the Balanced Scorecard to Ensure Investments and Impacts Are Kept in Equilibrium

Originated by Kaplan and Norton (see www.bscol.com/bscol/leadership), the value of a balanced scorecard approach is its focus on more than just financial expenditure and performance. So in addition to tracking financial elements (incorporating some form of ROI that makes sense for a nonprofit organization), it looks at the perspective of the customer or user and the impact that KM has on them. It looks at internal processes and the gains in efficiency and effectiveness that can be achieved. And it considers learning or growth by staff and the organization as a whole as the work unfolds so that the learning can contribute to improvements in KM to better support knowledge development, organization, sharing, and application.

The balanced scorecard comes the closest of any of the valuation methods to supporting the Foundation's results-based accountability framework (recall the trifecta of what did we do, how well did we do it, and is anyone better off?). It keeps financial considerations as part of the equation, but it does this in perspective with the what, how, and so what of the work. A Casey balanced scorecard suggests the challenges of sorting out the financial metrics (as discussed in the ROI section), and that thinking about

---

TEXT BOX 5.4. THE BALANCED SCORECARD

Core Components

Financial: What is the bottom line?
Customer: Is the organization meeting their needs?
Internal processes/structure: What is needed to do well to succeed?
Learning: How does the organization learn to meet its objectives?

processes, customers, and learning to further the work are better (but not necessarily easier) drivers to focus on and track when it comes to seeing change. Three and a half years into the initiative, Knowledge Services continues to adapt tools and processes that help Casey better address user needs. This is supported by a willingness to see learning itself as an important factor in the work, drawing on not only Casey's own direct experiences, but also what the Foundation is learning from other KM initiatives in philanthropy and elsewhere.

Taking the Pulse of the Organizational Culture: How Do Staff Think and Act Relative to the Foundation's Most Important Asset—Its Knowledge?

In *Knowledge Management: Challenges, Solutions, and Technologies* by Irma Becerra-Fernandez et al. (2004), the authors cite five components to an organization's infrastructure that influence how well knowledge management functions. They include the organization's culture, structure, physical environment, common or shared knowledge, and information technology infrastructure. Although all play a significant role, the organizational culture is perhaps the most compelling and influential when it comes to enabling or impeding KM.

Organizational culture reflects the values, norms, beliefs, and behavior of staff. It can influence how the organization functions as greatly as staff hierarchy, departmental units, and financial resources. In short, the culture of the workplace can embrace or destroy an initiative like KM.

A handful of indicators help inform where KM and the organizational culture is. First, Casey is a relatively open culture. People talk to each other, share information, and participate in a number of exchanges and forums within and across grant portfolios promoted by senior leadership. Periodic surveys of staff have indicated that most feel that the organization is doing a better job of organizing and sharing its resources internally than it used to. In fact, support for and contributions to the internal KM System and public Knowledge Center (both of which are web-based data warehouses) has been significant. The internal KM System started with 3,500 resources in mid-2004. Content three years later is now approaching 10,000 items. If Casey suffers from any challenge in this regard, it would be, to paraphrase Nancy Dixon (2004), that the staff has an asking problem, not a sharing problem. When Knowledge Services requested knowledge resources from staff to populate its internal and external KM Systems, nearly all responded positively and quickly, as evinced by the resource totals above. On the other hand, staff have not had the time or the inclination to seek out resources from the internal KM System, as measured by the number of visits to it, suggesting a culture dynamic (discussed later) or the view that informal networks and solutions suffice. However, the outside consultant engaged to do the KM study in 2002 underscored that the real challenge for an organization is to push knowledge public, where real needs and use of these products would stimulate demand and further knowledge development. To that end, Casey unveiled its new Knowledge Center (a public version of its KM System) in the spring of 2007 as part of a comprehensive website (www.aecf.org) overhaul.

Part of the KM life cycle entails the absorption, alignment, and integration of its language and tools with other work flows and processes. Organizational culture is slow to pick up new norms and behaviors, yet in the case of KM, this happens more easily when an organization already does KM-like things, but has not necessarily thought of them that way. Key to the organization accepting KM is for it to recognize and celebrate its preexisting KM-like tendencies and that new KM processes and procedures enhance rather than undermine what has come before. The strength-based approach of drawing on new KM tools and approaches to build on what is already happening can help take the work to a scope, scale, and efficiency that generate a strong return on investment. This takes time, patience, persistence, and the wisdom to know what to change and what to leave alone.

FACTORS INFLUENCING KM'S EARLY SUCCESSES AND CHALLENGES AT CASEY

A number of preexisting conditions and factors have helped positively shape the progress of KM at the Casey Foundation so far. First, the organization brought these preexisting conditions to the table: (1) a clear vision and set of goals and a perceived need that better knowledge and better shared knowledge would help the organization achieve its vision; (2) attributes of a learning environment (inquisitiveness, openness, a commitment to "making new mistakes," and a doggedness in search of evidence to inform its decisions); (3) a focus on outcomes or results-based thinking that provided a platform for theorizing, strategizing, implementation, and evaluation; and (4) a senior leadership predisposed toward and conversant with the elements of KM, (even if the formal elements of KM were new to them).

Several factors in the first years of KM have helped it move deeper into the KM life cycle than it has fared in other organizations. These included a significant investment in up-front thinking by the Foundation about KM, what it could accomplish at Casey, and how it might best be introduced and sustained. Another factor has been the organization's willingness to invest sufficient start-up funds to build web-based tools to organize, store, and make available the Foundation's knowledge resources. Room has also been given to allow the KM work to find itself and align and support the core programs of the Foundation, both by providing collateral support to these programs from the Knowledge Services unit and by identifying KM responsibilities that should reside within the programs themselves.

These circumstances have helped KM get traction in the Foundation. Early success to the initiative is substantiated in several ways. Acknowledgment of KM and a basic understanding of its role have grown over time. More Casey products are organized and centrally accessible than ever before, both on its internal KM System and on the new public Knowledge Center. Programs are more intentionally thinking about documenting meetings, workshops, and conferences and distributing the products. And the many pre-KM learning activities (consultative sessions, peer forums, field visits and sharings, etc.) continue and flourish.

Challenges do remain. The qualitative and quantitative metrics discussed earlier contribute only partially to a valuation that justifies to some the investment in staffing and technology in KM. The evaluation mantra—that we value what we can measure and what we cannot measure we don't value—inevitably drives some of the conversation around initiatives like KM. Others counter that not everything that is valuable can be assigned a value, and that not everything that we can count, counts. The fact is, it is hard to measure the value of KM, particularly in fields like philanthropy. Approaches beyond ROI help get around this by broadening the conversation and placing it in a larger organizational and mission context. If there is any advice to offer from Casey's experiences in KM, it is to take the longer view and to consider a range of measures when assessing its value and impact.

Another challenge in any long-term institutionalization of KM is the time and space problem. Short of being a formal part of staff performance measures or a reward/incentive program, staffers sometimes do not feel they are supported or authorized to take the time to carry out the core elements of KM. Finally, competing interests and resource constraints are common challenges that many organizational initiatives face. KM is no different and is occasionally challenged to hold its ground against more established programs. This can be exacerbated by its situation as a relatively new management approach, considered by some as a fad that can be waited out until another replaces it.

WHERE DO WE GO FROM HERE? KM FOR THE LONG HAUL

In the foundation world, support or affinity groups like the Council on Foundations (www.cof.org) or Grantmakers for Effective Organizations (www.geofunders.org) provide forums for funders to discuss effective strategies to increase their grantmaking impact. KM has been one approach among several that has received scrutiny and support when foundation experts come together to share their experiences coming out of the philanthropic sector's first generation of KM.

Two strands of thinking have emerged. First is that continuous improvement in KM through the exploration and application of new tools and approaches is and always will be an essential element. Technology improvements can help KM get better when it comes to capturing, organizing, and sharing knowledge. Collaborative engagements are equally important, so approaches like social network analysis, collaborative learning, peer networking, and communities of practice are essential when it comes to moving the conversation from creating products to their sharing and application.

A second strand draws on the value of these individual continuous improvement efforts and goes further by anchoring KM in the broader notion of organizational learning. Although historically somewhat problematic for some organizations to adopt because of its abstract nature, organizational learning contributes the "so what?" question to any KM initiative. In other words, why is the organization investing in knowledge management? For what purpose are we creating, organizing, and disseminating knowledge? This helps place KM in the larger context of what an organization is trying to accomplish (its hoped-for outcomes) and how KM can help. It reminds us that the work we care about has meaning only when it is lifted up out of research and data bases and systems and is embodied in the stakeholders that are intently working with one another to make a difference.

NOTE

The opinions expressed by the author in this chapter are not necessarily those of the Annie E. Casey Foundation.

REFERENCES

Becerra-Fernandez, Irma, A. Gonzalez, and R. Sabherwal. 2004. *Knowledge Management: Challenges, Solutions, and Technologies.* Upper Saddle River, NJ: Pearson/Prentice Hall.
Dixon, Nancy. 2004. "Does Your Organization Have an Asking Problem?" *KM Review* 7 (2).
O'Dell, Carla. 2000. *Road Map to Knowledge Management Results.* Houston, TX: American Productivity and Quality Center.

6

Shipyard Planning Case

Tom Housel, Eric Tarantino,
Sandra Hom, and Johnathan Mun

BACKGROUND ON THE HISTORY OF THE ORGANIZATION

The United States Navy recently initiated a focus on how best to manage its many knowledge resources, in people and information technology. To whit, a new designation of knowledge manager was created. These officers have been charged with responsibility for ensuring a positive return on investment in the navy's large investments in information technology. As such, they have been active in establishing, leading, and participating in knowledge management (KM) projects at the "point of the spear" (front-line war fighting efforts) and in routine operations. One of the more routine operational contexts for KM efforts has been in evaluating the use of collaborative tools for improving utilization of knowledge assets across core processes such as ship maintenance, modernization, and repair. This case is an example of how the use of new metrics to evaluate the potential of collaborative and three-dimensional visualization tools will impact the navy's ship alteration (i.e., modernization, repair, and maintenance) planning processes.

Private and public (i.e., naval) shipyards support the modernization, repair, and maintenance of large seagoing vessels such as aircraft carriers, submarines, and cruise ships. Over the past fifty years, there has been a significant reduction in the number of shipyards available in the United States to support these activities. The reduced capacity of the remaining four public and six private shipyards limits their ability to deal with expanding commitments. It is therefore necessary that they become more efficient and effective in a continued effort to reduce costs and maintain defense capabilities.

Planning yards provide the essential service of supporting the navy shipyards' primary servicing functions. They plan for ship alterations in advance of the actual modernization, repair, or maintenance efforts. As a component of the navy's Fleet Modernization Program, the planning yard receives funding along with technical guidance and tasking orders to prepare the shipyards to complete any task mandated by the Department of the Navy (DoN). The planning yard's goal is to minimize system or human work schedule conflicts to ensure ship alterations (SHIPALTs) proceed as efficiently as possible.

Planning-yard activities involve seven sequential processes constituting the overall SHIPALT planning process, including:

1. issue tasking
2. interpret orders
3. plan for ship check
4. conduct ship check
5. report assembly
6. revise schedule
7. generate drawings

This chain of processes is executed for every vessel as it approaches its shipyard availability period and includes numerous subprocesses.

The schedule, timeline, and location for ship availabilities are established by navy leadership far in advance, but calendar dates and work assigned may be constrained by budget allowances and other prioritization factors. Availability schedules may also be affected by specific trigger events that prompt major changes in the deployment of naval forces, such as the terrorist attacks of September 11, 2001, and Operation Iraqi Freedom. These events resulted in an ultimate surging to deploy seven carrier battle groups and the largest amphibious task group assembled since World War II.

Planning yards produce standard SHIPALT planning documents that can be considered their final products or "outputs." These documents include two-dimensional (2D) detailed AUTOCAD (automated computer-aided design) drawings of ship compartments, installation areas, and equipment-removal routes, as well as material lists that support maintenance and modernization plans. Planning yards also provide less tangible services, for example, ensuring alteration-specific capacities, such as sufficient "chillwater" for air conditioning or increased electrical capacity, meet the requirements for a given SHIPALT.

PROJECT/CASE DESCRIPTION

The focus of this case is to estimate the potential value that would be added to the planning yard function by three-dimensional visualization technology and a product life cycle management collaborative tool. Specifically, this project analyzed how the technologies could impact the return on investment (ROI) of this core process while quantifying the value and risk of the new options these technologies would provide the leadership of the navy shipyard planning process.

The knowledge value-added (KVA) + real options (RO) framework was used to complete this analysis. KVA provides a means for generating ROI estimates based on the market comparables valuation[1] of planning yard processes. These estimates also provide the discounted cash-flow estimates as inputs for the real options valuation analysis projections.

There is a high demand for this kind of valuation analysis, given the costliness of the navy's current maintenance and modernization programs. In the 2005 fiscal year alone, the navy spent $3.9 billion on fleet maintenance and modernization efforts; these are challenging efforts entailing labor-intensive and costly planning yard functions. In addition, many of the navy's ships were designed and fabricated in the 1970s and 1980s with primarily two-dimensional (2D) drawings and no comprehensive, centralized digital data layer to store and organize the necessary documentation. Upon realizing the potential for improvement, naval leadership contacted our KVA+RO team to help identify and build the business case for process reengineering.

Commercial off-the-shelf (COTS) technologies like three-dimensional terrestrial laser scanning visualization (3DVis) (see figure 6.1) and collabo-

Figure 6.1.   Three-Dimensional Terrestrial Laser Scanning Equipment

Figure 6.2. Sample Point Cloud Image (USNS Ship Exterior)

rative Product Lifecycle Management (PLM) software could improve maintenance and modernization efforts while reducing costs. COTS technologies could complement current naval maintenance initiatives, including the SHIPMAIN initiative—"one shipyard for the nation."[2]

The outputs of the 3DVis technology provides a three-dimensional point cloud (see figure 6.2) that provides contractors working on SHIPALTs a precise rendering of the dimensions of the hull where the alteration will take place as well as a historical record of the alteration. This electronic image can then be shared, via collaborative PLM software, with anyone involved in the SHIPALT planning process, as well as those downstream who must actually perform the alteration.

The current project began to uncover the possibilities afforded by introducing 3DVis and collaborative PLM technologies into the navy's maintenance and modernization efforts by analyzing the process of planning for a SHIPALT. The methodology establishes evidence that suggests reengineering the shipyard planning yard processes will shorten the duration of navy ship time in port, while reducing the annual operating cost of four government planning yards by more than $30 million.

RETURN ON INVESTMENT/VALUATION METHODS USED

The KVA+RO framework measures operating performance, cost-effectiveness, return on investment, risk, strategic flexibility, and analytical portfolio optimization. The framework facilitates regulatory compliance and applies portfolio management techniques to evaluate programs and risks while taking into account the uncertainty inherent in estimating future benefits. Large, complex organizations ranging from publicly traded *Fortune* 500 firms to public-sector entities can use the KVA+RO framework. Its focus on core processes, subprocesses, and outputs provides several advantages:

- Quantifies the value of specific processes, functions, information technology, departments, divisions, or organizations in common units.
- Provides historical data on costs and revenues of specific processes and tasks of specific programs or organizations.
- Facilitates regulatory compliance in the public sector (with legislation such as the Clinger-Cohen Act of 1996) mandating portfolio management for all federal agencies. In the private sector, facilitates compliance with Sarbanes-Oxley by making performance among corporate entities more transparent.
- Highlights operational efficiencies and inefficiencies.
- Leverages current and potential portfolio investments by estimating potential total value created.

The KVA+RO framework helps organizations understand the specific process resources involved in the production of an output, the cost of each process, and its contribution to the bottom line. Government entities can use the framework to enhance existing performance tools, while corporate leadership can utilize it to value specific divisions or operating units in their efforts to determine division profitability or shareholder value.

The KVA+RO framework is also designed to help organizations manage information technology (IT) investments and mitigate risk. The framework's three components of KVA data collection, ratio analysis, and RO analysis provide performance-based data and analyses on individual projects, programs, and processes within a portfolio of IT investments.

The first step in the KVA+RO framework is KVA data collection on the processes required to produce an output. For public organizations, once all process data is accurately documented, the data is subjected to market comparables analysis to establish surrogate revenue estimates and establish "as-is" baseline estimates. The KVA methodology is then applied to estimate the value and historical costs of each process. In the second step, cost per unit of output calculated by KVA, in conjunction with price-per-unit estimates, provides the raw data required for ROI ratio analysis. In the final step of the framework, risk-based simulation and RO analysis are conducted to estimate the future value and risks of potential investments, as well as the best strategic pathway to proceed. Several possible scenarios are evaluated, enabling decision makers to assess risk, leverage uncertainty, and limit downside risk.

KVA assumes that humans and technology in organizations add value by taking inputs and changing them into outputs through core processes. The amount of outputs a process produces can be a measure of value or benefit. It is also necessary to assume that:

- It is possible to describe all process outputs in common units (i.e., the knowledge required to produce the outputs) allowing historical revenue and cost data to be assigned to those processes at any given point in time designated for the analysis.
- All outputs can be described in terms of the time required to learn how to produce them from a common learner point of reference (i.e., Joe Smith would learn how to produce all the outputs for every single process).
- Learning Time, a surrogate for the knowledge required to produce process outputs, is measured in common units of time. Consequently, Units of Learning Time − Common Units of Output (K).
- Establishing a common unit of output makes it possible to compare all outputs in terms of cost per unit as well as price per unit, because revenue can now be assigned at the suborganizational level.
- Once cost and revenue streams have been assigned to suborganizational outputs, normal accounting, financial performance, and profitability metrics can be applied.

Describing processes in common units permits market-comparable data to be generated, which is particularly important for nonprofits like the U.S. Navy. Using a market comparables approach, data from the commercial sector can be used to estimate price per common unit, allowing for surrogate revenue estimates of process outputs for nonprofits. This provides a common-units basis to define benefit streams, regardless of which process is analyzed. KVA differs from other nonprofit ROI models, because it allows for revenue estimates, enabling the use of traditional accounting, financial performance, and profitability measures at the suborganizational level.

Aggregate productivity estimates are captured in two key performance ratios: return on investment and return on knowledge (ROK). While ROI is the traditional financial ratio (i.e., [revenue − cost] / cost), ROK (i.e., revenue / cost) identifies how a specific process converts existing knowledge into outputs so decision makers can quantify costs and measure value derived from investments in human and technology resources. A higher ROK signifies better utilization of knowledge resources. If IT investments do not improve the ROK value of a given process, steps must be taken to improve that process's function and performance via changes to the IT-human resource mix.

Potential strategic investments can then be forecasted with RO analysis using the KVA data. RO analysis is a robust and analytical process incorporating the risk identification (applying various sensitivity techniques), risk quantification (applying Monte Carlo simulation), risk valuation (applying

RO analysis), risk mitigation (utilizing RO framing), and risk diversification (employing analytical portfolio optimization).

As a financial valuation tool, RO helps organizational leadership adapt decisions to respond to unexpected environmental or market developments. RO can be used to:

- identify different corporate investment decision pathways or projects that management can consider in highly uncertain business conditions.
- value the feasibility and financial viability of each strategic decision pathway.
- prioritize pathways or projects based on qualitative and quantitative metrics.
- optimize strategic investment decisions by elevating different decision paths under certain conditions or determine how a different sequence of pathways can lead to the optimal strategy.
- time the execution of investments and find the optimal trigger values and cost or revenue drivers.
- manage existing, or develop new, options and strategic decision pathways for future opportunities.

Although there are many approaches to RO, the methodology used in the KVA+RO valuation framework was developed by Dr. Johnathan Mun.[3] Dr. Mun's KVA+RO approach consists of the eight steps, which are listed in figure 6.3.

The strategic value of KVA+RO for the Department of Defense (DoD) is that it offers a way to objectively quantify the value of alternative decision pathways or courses of action for decision makers. In a dynamic and uncertain environment where investment decisions must be flexible and fluid, strategic real options may offer insights into alternative paths and how they relate to unique DoD requirements. KVA+RO is primarily a tool set to augment existing performance tools and can be applied to organizations at almost any level of detail.

WHAT ACTUALLY HAPPENED WITH THE PROJECT

KVA+RO analysis was applied to the Puget Sound Planning Yard. Specifically, this project applied the methodology to the ship alteration planning process in an attempt to demonstrate how reengineered planning yard processes could positively affect the navy's maintenance and modernization efforts. COTS technologies, including three-dimensional laser scanning and collaborative PLM solutions, were evaluated under three scenarios: current "as-is," potential "to-be," and "radical-to-be." The "as-is" model represented the current, baseline planning process. The "to-be" model represented the potential influence of 3DVis technology on the

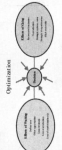

Figure 6.3. Integrated Risk Analysis Approach

planning process. The "radical-to-be" model represented the impact of both 3DVis and collaborative PLM technologies on model parameters.

The initial data collection involved group interview meetings with five planning yard subject matter experts from the Bremerton, Washington, shipyard as well as current employees of Puget Sound Planning Yard. Together, these experts described the seven sequential core processes that encompass all planning yard work (see figure 6.4).

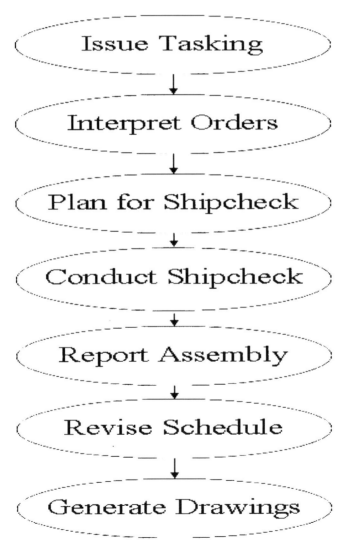

Figure 6.4.   Planning Yard Core Processes

The three scenario evaluations indicated that the COTS technologies could significantly improve the planning yard processes. The technologies could increase the overall value of the maintenance processes while reducing costs over the twenty-, thirty-, and fifty-year life cycle of navy ships. Digital 3DVis data capture, with its high-quality, accurate, and reusable outputs, in conjunction with information storage and sharing capabilities of a collaborative PLM tool suite, has the potential to provide significantly more value over current processes.

Specific benefits include:

- Reduced maintenance costs for ships by expediting maintenance work in shipyards (see table 6.1).
- Decreased maintenance costs by eliminating or reducing the number of DoD planning yard employee workdays for the two processes (see table 6.2).
- Improved fleet utilization and/or reduced fleet inventory requirements through reduced cycle time: Shipyard planning process duration could be reduced by 50 percent. More importantly, if every operational navy ship was available one additional week for tasking over a two-year time span, the navy would have 280 additional weeks for tasking assignments, training, or crew rest and relaxation opportunities.
- Reduced inventory and expanded capability: Expediting the planning process creates a ripple effect through all industrial activities for maintenance and modernization of naval assets. Increasing the duration of ship availabilities and providing more operational availability of naval assets could provide additional options in deploying more ships or reducing the size of the fleet. Increased time gaps could be scheduled between new ship acquisitions, or ship decommissioning could be allowed to occur at an earlier date.
- Increased net value and productivity in current shipyard planning processes would allow for increased shipboard modernization.

The performance of the seven core planning processes (see table 6.3) indicated that there were discontinuities among the process ROIs. To obtain these ROIs, market comparables were used to estimate the surrogate revenue for the outputs of these processes by establishing a common price per unit of output. All ROI estimates used the same baseline price per unit of output even though this figure would likely change over time due to normal inflationary pressures, changes in the market, and so on. However, because the estimate was based on a very stable and mature business segment, that is, ship maintenance, modernization, and repair, it was deemed reasonable to use the same referent point price per common unit of output for the two "to-be" models.

Table 6.1. Potential Costs and Cost Savings

	Process Title	"AS-IS"	"TO-BE"	"RADICAL-TO-BE"	"AS-IS" & "TO-BE" Cost Savings	"AS-IS" & "RADICAL" Cost Savings
1	ISSUE TASKING	$173,500	$173,500	$173,500	$0	$0
2	INTERPRET ORDERS	$520,000	$520,000	$328,000	$0	$192,000
3	PLAN FOR SHIPCHECK	$1,655,000	$714,000	$374,500	$941,000	$1,280,500
4	CONDUCT SHIPCHECK	$2,604,500	$1,364,000	$1,041,000	$1,240,500	$1,563,500
5	REPORT ASSEMBLY	$235,000	$235,000	$122,000	$0	$113,000
6	REVISE SCHEDULE	$131,000	$131,000	$131,000	$0	$0
7	GENERATE DRAWINGS	$39,386,000	$4,716,000	$2,319,000	$34,670,000	$37,067,000
	TOTALS	$44,705,000	$7,853,500	$4,489,000	$36,851,5000	$40,216,000

Table 6.2. Human Resource Requirements

	(No. of Workdays)		
	"AS-IS"	*"TO-BE"*	*"RADICAL-TO-BE"*
Conduct Shipcheck	286	145	113
Generate Drawings	3960	521	256

After the KVA analysis was completed, real options analysis was performed to determine the prospective value of three basic options over a three-year period with the KVA data as a platform. The three potential strategies are presented below in the strategy tree (figure 6.5). The "to-be" potential pathway for implementing 3D scanning technology utilized a stage gate sequential compound option, meaning that implementation would be divided into several stages and the success of each stage would be dependent on the success of the previous stage. This would allow for the 3D technology to be tested in a proof-of-concept stage at the Puget Sound shipyard instead of immediately throughout all shipyards. The technology would only be implemented at the remaining shipyards if the proof of concept was successful. The options to abandon and to defer capital investments until risk and uncertainty is resolved create higher value because it hedges the risk of a large-scale implementation.

The "radical-to-be" strategy is similar to the to-be approach, because it too uses a sequential compound option, but combines the implementation of the 3D scanning technology with the PLM collaborative technologies. However, it also takes into consideration the fact that these technologies will be useful in other segments of modernization and maintenance, providing additional expansion and growth options that increase the value of this strategic path.

Table 6.3. Shipyard Planning Return on Investment

Core Process	Process Title	*"AS-IS"* ROI	*"TO-BE"* ROI	*"RADICAL-TO-BE"* ROI
1	**Issue Tasking**	−69%	−69%	−68%
2	**Interpret Orders**	518%	881%	1168%
3	**Plan for Shipcheck**	−99%	−96%	−92%
4	**Conduct Shipcheck**	552%	1785%	2530%
5	**Report Assembly**	838%	838%	1601%
6	**Revise Schedule**	1374%	1374%	1374%
7	**Generate Drawings**	−37%	2169%	4515%

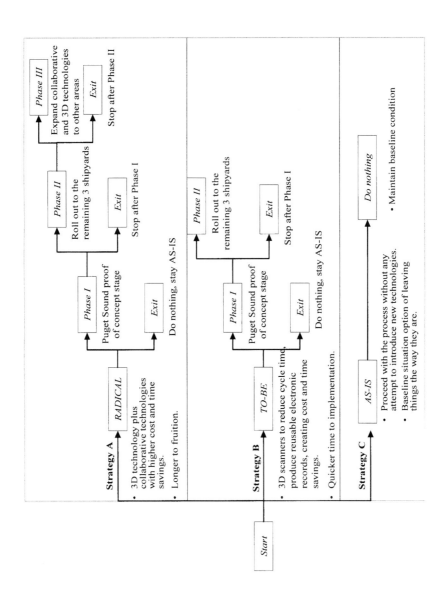

Figure 6.5. Course of Action Strategic Options

Table 6.4.   Real Options Analysis

	Strategic Option Valuation		
	"As-Is"	"To-Be"	"Radical-To-Be"
Benefits	$49,175,537	$93,344,192	$95,097,452
Costs	$44,705,033	$ 7,853,206	$ 4,488,888
Total Strategic Value	$ 4,470,503	$87,227,330	$91,601,502
Factor Improvement		**19.51**	**20.49**
	Expansion Valuation on Stage-Gate Options		
	"As-Is"	"To-Be"	"Radical-To-Be"
Benefits	$147,526,610	$280,032,576	$950,974,520
Costs	$134,115,100	$ 23,562,618	$ 44,888,877
Long-Term Total Strategic Value	$ 13,411,510	$265,742,275	$923,752,800
Factor Improvement		**19.81**	**68.88**

Results from running the different scenarios seen in figure 6.5 are as follows:

- To-be and radical-to-be provide highest overall total strategic value with little difference between the two (19.51 to 20.49 times improvement over the baseline as-is option). (See table 6.4.)
- When considering all the downstream options available from collaborative technologies with 3D scanning and PLM capabilities, radical-to-be is the optimal option, providing an overwhelming 68.88 times the value from the existing as-is base case (see table 6.4).

SUCCESSES AND FAILURES

As evidenced from the improvement in many process ROIs, 3DVis and collaborative technologies, when combined, have the greatest potential for improving the maintenance, modernization, and repair planning process. As is the case within the planning yard environment, if the 3DVis data and documents related to planning work were broadly utilized, they would be stored as reference data in a common ship alteration database and would be instantly available to shipyard engineers as well as the contractors who would have to make estimates for their costs to perform the alterations. With this new capability, engineers and contractors would have the ability to electronically communicate with different experts when needed, view installation drawings, and consider a SHIPALT's manufacturability and material availability much earlier in the planning process. In this context, the collaborative PLM tools would improve efforts to view, edit, and analyze SHIPALT-pertinent data while allowing all stakeholders to track work progress and stay abreast of changes.

The "success" of this project is that it provides decision makers with defendable estimates of the potential ROI in these two technologies. These estimates supplemented the decision maker's intuitive understanding that these technologies would benefit the navy's maintenance and modernization efforts.

The "failure" of this project is its limited scope. Obviously, there needs to be much more work in deciding how to take maximum advantage of the potential of these technologies throughout the entire ship maintenance, repair, and modernization life cycle. This research did not cover any specifics of repair planning or material assessment, nor did it reach beyond the planning phase into the realm of production. The reader should bear in mind that any benefits or return on investment demonstrated by this project only begins to uncover the potential of IT in the much larger shipyard industry.

Finally, although this research demonstrates the potential benefits, it has not led to direct action to date. The analysis has, however, stimulated much discussion and has virtually ensured the inclusion of these two technologies within Phase IV and V (these two phases cover the planning and implementation of ship alterations) of the new SHIPMAIN initiative. In addition, to really reap the benefits of these potential improvements, the performance of these systems must be tracked over time to ensure success. In this context, the navy has nearly completed the purchase of a KVA performance accounting system site license called GaussSoft, which will make this monitoring feasible.

EPILOGUE

This proof-of-concept case study reveals the potential value select IT resources may have for the U.S. Navy shipyard planning process. Digital 3DVis, with its quality, accuracy, and reusable outputs, when combined with the capabilities of PLM collaborative software, has the promise of dramatically increasing the productivity of the naval ship maintenance and modernization efforts. Moreover, these technologies have the potential to provide tremendous value in most of the core processes of the U.S. shipbuilding and repair industry. Given war-strained budgets, rising shipbuilding costs, and reduced ship acquisitions by the navy, industry consolidation and shrinkage will continue, which will greatly impact the nation's security options. These technologies present an opportunity to help the United States maintain its naval national security requirements and allow the industry to remain competitive in the global arena.

The case also demonstrates the usefulness of the KVA+RO methodology in examining DoD investment options. Monetizing outputs as well as inputs provides a means to compare various options that, on the surface, do not appear to be comparable. Such a methodology may prove useful in helping DoD and industry leaders analyze alternative acquisition trade-off decisions.

NOTES

1. Market comparables valuation is further described in Tom Housel and Arthur A. Bell's book, *Measuring and Managing Knowledge* (Boston: McGraw-Hill/Irwin, 2001).

2. Launched in 2002, SHIPMAIN's goal is to ensure that all shipyard processes are redesigned, with consistency among different maintenance facilities, to preserve ship quality and lifespan within schedule constraints. Navy leadership anticipates that SHIPMAIN will ultimately reduce the overall cost of ship maintenance and modernization by establishing a common planning process for surface ship alterations. By establishing a disciplined management process with objective measurements, SHIPMAIN strives to increase the efficiency of the process without compromising its effectiveness. Finally, the initiative will institutionalize the process and implement a continuous improvement method.

3. See his book, *Real Options Analysis: Tools and Techniques for Valuing Strategic Investments and Decisions* (New York: John Wiley & Sons, 2002), which is in widespread use in MBA programs nationally and internationally.

REFERENCES

Balisle, P. M., and T. W. Lafleur. 2003. "Reengineering for a Culture of Readiness." *Sea Power*. Available from http://musrv.spear.navy.mil/maintu/ShipMain/ShipMain Gram_Intro.doc (retrieved October 10, 2005).

Browning, M. 2005. "Executive Suite: Putting the Clinger-Cohen Act in Perspective." *Government Computer News* 24. Available from www.gcn.com/24_15/project-management/36103-1.html (retrieved fall, 2005).

Chief of Naval Operations. 2003. *Maintenance Policy for U.S. Navy Ships.* OPNAV INSTRUCTION 4700.7K. Retrieved September 1, 2005, from http://neds.daps.dla.mil/Directives/4700_7k.pdf.

DoD (Department of Defense). 2004. *DoD Maintenance, Policy, Programs and Resources FACT BOOK.* Washington, DC: Office of the Deputy Under Secretary of Defense.

———. 2003. DoD Directive 5000.1. (May 12) *The Defense Acquisition System.* Available from www.dtic.mil (retrieved summer, 2005).

Federation of American Scientists. n.d. Alteration. In *ISR Glossary of Terms.* Available from www.fas.org/man/dod-101/sys/ship/docs/rept21a.htm (retrieved October 30, 2005).

Gallaher, P., and J. O'Rourke. 2004. *Effective Use of Collaborative Information Technology to Enhance Group Performance.* Master's thesis, Naval Postgraduate School, 5–7.

Greaves, T. 2005. "3D Laser Scanning Market Red Hot: 2005 Forecast Raised to $178 Million; 45% Growth Projected." *SparView* 3. Available from www.sparlic.com (retrieved October 12, 2005).

Housel, T. J., and A. H. Bell. 2001. "Measuring Return on Knowledge." In *Measuring and Managing Knowledge*, 91–107. San Francisco: McGraw-Hill Higher Education.

International Engineering Consortium. 2005. *Knowledge Value-Added (KVA) Methodology*. Chicago, IL: International Engineering Consortium. Available from www.iec.org/online/tutorials/kva/ (retrieved spring, 2005).

Klemm, W. R. 2002. *The Lessons Learned—Times Four: America's Public Shipyards Deliver Quality Fleet Support*. Arlington, VA: Navy League of the United States. Available from www.navyleague.org (retrieved October 16, 2005).

McKeen, J. D., and H. A. Smith. 2003. *Making IT Happen, Critical Issues in IT Management*. Chichester, UK:: John Wiley & Sons.

Mun, J. 2002. *Real Options Analysis: Tools and Techniques for Valuing Strategic Investments and Decisions*. New York: John Wiley & Sons.

National Shipbuilding Research Program (NSRP). 2005. *Ship Check Data Capture*. Available from www.nsrp.org/projects/shipcheck.pdf (retrieved spring, 2005).

Spatial Integrated Systems. Available from www.sisinc.org. (retrieved spring, 2005).

Tate, R. *NDE Ship Change Document (SCD) Now Operational in Support of SHIPMAIN Alterations and Modernization Entitled Process*. Available from www.fmp.navy.mil/FMPACTIVE/BusinessPolicy/FMPDocuments/Documents/Shipmainentitledocs/SHIPMAINinNDE.pdf (retrieved November 5, 2005).

UGS. *Transforming the Process of Innovation*. Available from www.ugs.com (retrieved summer, 2005).

U.S. Congress. House. 2005. Statement of Rear Admiral Mark A. Hugel deputy director for fleet readiness, Staff of the Chief of Naval Operations, before the House Armed Services Committee Subcommittee on Readiness.

U.S. General Accounting Office. 2004. *Defense Logistics: GAO's Observations on Maintenance Aspects of the Navy's Fleet Response Plan*. H.R. Rep. No. GAO-04-724R. Available from www.gao.gov/htext/d04724r.html (retrieved November 20, 2005).

U.S. Navy. 2002. *FMP Business Policy/Process*. Available from www.fmp.navy.mil (retrieved August, 2005).

APPENDIX 6.1

Column Descriptions

The following list describes the purpose of each column of the ship alteration planning process in table 6.5. Furthermore, an example of each column follows the description. Each example is drawn from process 1 or "Issue Tasking."

1. # Org

The "# Org" column is a constant and simply accounts for the four public naval shipyards. However, when estimating the impact on commercial shipyards, this number may not be a constant. Since there are four public shipyards, the "# Org" for process 1 is "4."

2. Est. # Shipcheck per Org

The "Est. # Shipcheck per Org" column represents the average amount of shipchecks per shipyard per year. To remain conservative, and to properly account for planning yard work outsourced to private industry, this study approximates that work across the four public planning yards amounts to 40 shipchecks per year or 10 per shipyard per year. This is an average, but the actual number of shipchecks for each planning yard can be substituted to measure the performance of given shipyards. In this example, since there are 10 shipchecks per shipyard per year the estimated shipchecks per org for process 1 is "10."

3. Head Count per Shipcheck

The "Head Count per Shipcheck" column represents the number of employees assigned to complete the given process for each cycle, or iteration. Two people are involved in process 1 so the head count is simply "2."

4. Times Fired per Shipcheck

The estimate for "Times Fired per Shipcheck" is the aggregated number of occurrences of each process by public-sector planning yards, per shipcheck. This value was achieved by looking at statistical information for fiscal years 2003, 2004, and 2005, and by considering the estimates provided by the subject matter experts at Puget Sound Planning Yard. It is reasonable to use the shipcheck as a method to establish the total firings of each process, because the shipcheck precipitates the other processes. In other words, counting shipchecks provides the multiplier for the firings of the other processes. For

Table 6.5. KVA Analysis of "As-Is" Ship Alteration Planning Process

Values Reflect Estimates for all U.S. Public-Sector Planning Yards

Core Process	Process Title	# Org	Est. # Shipcheck per Org	Head Count per Shipcheck	Times Fired per Shipcheck	Time (days)	Daily Salary	% IT	ALT	K in IT
1	Issue Tasking	4	10	2	1	8	$271.10	30	572	172
2	Interpret Orders	4	10	5	100	10	$226.20	13	393	52
3	Plan for Shipcheck	4	10	35	1	6	$226.20	5	211	11
4	Conduct Shipcheck	4	10	35	40	10	$271.10	18	4,980	896
5	Report Assembly	4	10	1	1	6	$226.20	5	29,055	1,453
6	Revise Schedule	4	10	1	1	3	$226.20	41	18,954	7,771
7	Generate Drawings	4	10	110+	500	18	$226.20	11	618	68

Continued . . .

Core Process	Process Title	TLT	Rank Order	Total Knowledge	% Knowledge	Revenue	Total Cost	ROK	ROI
1	Issue Tasking	744	5	29,744	0.11	$53,716	$173,500	31%	−69%
2	Interpret Orders	445	4	1,780,141	6.54	$3,214,826	$520,000	618%	518%
3	Plan for Shipcheck	222	3	8,862	0.03	$16,004	$1,655,000	1%	−99%
4	Conduct Shipcheck	5,878	6	9,402,240	34.53	$16,979,870	$2,604,500	652%	552%
5	Report Assembly	30,508	2	1,220,310	4.48	$2,203,805	$235,000	938%	838%
6	Revise Schedule	26,725	1	1,069,006	3.93	$1,930,559	$131,000	1474%	1,374%
7	Generate Drawings	686	7	13,719,600	50.38	$24,776,758	$39,386,000	63%	−37%
	"AS-IS" PROCESS TOTALS:					**$49,175,537**	**$44,705,000**	**110%**	**10%**

example, process x fires 10 times per shipcheck, while process y fires 5 times per shipcheck. Process 1 fires once per shipcheck so the entry is simply "1."

5. Time (Days)

The estimated amount of days personnel spend on each subprocess. It takes 8 days to fire process 1.

6. Daily Salary

The salary each member of personnel earns per day. The daily salary of those involved in process 1 is $271.10.

7. % IT

Each process contains a certain degree of process automation that can be expressed in terms of the percentage to which the process is automated by information technology (IT). It is important to estimate precisely how much of each subprocess is automated, and to be consistent in those estimates, so that the knowledge embedded in the IT resources is accounted for. The percentage IT estimate is factored into the Total Learning Time (TLT) estimate. Subject matter experts estimate that 30 percent of process 1 is automated.

8. ALT

In order to determine the actual learning time (ALT) from a common point of reference learner, the subject matter experts were instructed to imagine a baseline individual (e.g., Joe Smith) who has earned a college degree. All experts understood that each process learning time estimate must adhere to the basic assumptions that knowledge is only counted if in use, and the most succinct path to obtain a process output should be used for all estimates. It is estimated that process 1 takes 572 days to learn.

9. K in IT

Knowledge in information technology (K in IT) is a rough-cut estimate of the amount of output (or knowledge) produced by automation (IT). It is calculated by multiplying the "% IT" column by the "ALT" column. For process 1, when these two columns are multiplied, the resulting K in IT is 172.

10. TLT

A combination of ALT and the learning time derived from estimates of % IT are summed to arrive at the total learning time (TLT) for each process.

This is a surrogate for the time it would take to teach the common reference point learner (Joe Smith) all the tasks involved in the process including those performed by IT. Combining the ALT estimate and the amount of IT involved in process 1, you get a TLT of 744 days.

11. Rank Order

The subject matter experts rank-ordered each process in terms of its complexity to learn, independently of their estimates for actual learning times. Because perception of process complexity can vary, the exercise was conducted in a manner to minimize peer interaction and influence. In the ranking process, the number one (1) represents the core process considered the least complex and easiest to learn, while the number seven (7) represents the most complex and difficult to learn. All processes are ranked in between accordingly. The purpose of obtaining the rank order is to correlate these estimates with the actual learning time estimates to determine the level of reliability of the learning time estimates. A priori it is assumed that the two estimates should be highly correlated since they represent the same underlying phenomenon. The values in the ALT column must correlate well with the rank order numbers. Achieving a correlation result greater than 0.80 is considered sufficient, and ALT estimates should be accepted for all further calculations. The level of correlation for the two in the "as-is" scenario was 0.84. Process 1 was relatively difficult to learn, so it received a rank of "5."

12. Total Knowledge

"Total Knowledge" representes the amount of knowledge embedded in each process, which is also the total number of common units of output for the process. It is calculated by multiplying the "# Org," "Est. # Shipcheck per Org," "Times Fired per Shipcheck," and "TLT" columns. If you calculate the total knowledge for process 1 by the equation above, you get 29,744.

13. % Knowledge

The "% Knowledge" column is simply the percent of knowledge each process contributes to the overall ship alteration planning process. Process 1 provides 0.11 percent of the total knowledge.

14. Revenue

"Revenue" is calculated by multiplying the price-per-knowledge unit by the "Total Knowledge" column. The price-per-knowledge unit is calculated by taking the total revenue for the entire ship alteration process and dividing by the total amount of knowledge embedded in the process. The total revenue was calculated using a market-comparables contractor pre-mium approach. In this case, the market premium to pay a contractor to do the same jobs as the GS employees is approximately 10 percent higher. When the "% Knowledge" column is multiplied by the price per knowl-edge unit, you find that process 1 earns $53,716, which is 0.11 percent of the total revenue.

15. Total Cost

The collection of cost-related information was relatively simple, since in-formation on human capital cost for government employees is public in-formation. For cost calculations, the 2005 GS salary pay table was refer-enced. Since various steps and slight differences in pay exist within each GS rank, salary figures are based on the midpoint average pay of GS-12 plan-ning yard employees ($62,353/year) and GS-11 employees ($52,025/year). It was determined that most planning yard processes executed are accom-plished by personnel within these rank levels. Research also indicates that Puget Sound carries a more mature work force than other shipyards; there-fore, in this instance cost estimates were based on what was known to exist at the Puget Sound location. Also, because basic computing hardware and software was utilized in every scenario, IT cost is not included in the "as-is" analysis. It is assumed that each employee in this process has an email ac-count, laptop or desktop computer with identical software, and access to a printer. Material, travel, and other miscellaneous costs are not included in this analysis so labor cost may be isolated because they have the most im-pact on the variability of the cost of the process when automation is taken into account. The estimated total cost for process 1 is $173,500.

16. ROK

"ROK" is the return on knowledge and is calculated by dividing revenue by cost. Calculating the ROK for process 1, it equals 31 percent.

17. ROI

"ROI" provides the return on investment for each process and is calcu-lated by dividing (revenue − cost) by cost. When you calculate the return on investment for process 1 it equals −69 percent.

Key Assumptions

All shipcheck-related processes can vary in number, manpower require-ments, duration, and complexity. To account for these discrepancies many interview sessions were conducted with planning yard subject matter experts in person, via teleconference, or through email, and the following assumptions were made:

- Between the four public-sector planning yards, 40 shipchecks are accomplished. Other naval shipchecks are outsourced to private planning yards.
- The level of effort for each shipcheck is 100 SHIPALTs.
- All estimates assume a SHIPALT of medium-complexity.
- Each shipcheck team averages 35 personnel.
- The duration of a shipcheck is 10 workdays, with a travel day at each end.
- For each SHIPALT, at least 5 sketches/drawings are created.
- For each SHIPALT, approximately 10 digital photographs are captured.
- Each SHIPCHECK will have 5 Lead Codes, and many Follow Codes.

7

Knowledge Management and Competitive Intelligence for Strategic Decision Making

A Case Study of a Legal Information Services Firm in Canada

Kimiz Dalkir

THE ORGANIZATION: SOQUIJ

SOQUIJ (*Société québécoise d'information juridique*, or the Quebec Society for Legal Information), founded in 1976, promotes the research, processing, and development of legal information in order to improve its quality and accessibility. SOQUIJ is mandated by the National Assembly of the Province of Québec and is under the jurisdiction of the Quebec Department of Justice. SOQUIJ publishes decisions from the legal and administrative tribunals of the province of Québec. "Its high value-added products as commercialized in paper format (case-law reports, newletters, etc.) and electronic format (Internet-based case-law databanks) are provided to the legal, business and labour communities."[1]

SOQUIJ is self-financed through the sale of its products and services, including such flagship products as:

1) AZIMUT, Online Legal Information System: With its Juris.doc service, offers the largest selection of Québec jurisprudence through its Internet-based databanks. Users can search through full-text decisions or summaries, as well as through computerized court dockets.
2) Jugements.qc.ca: An online site SOQUIJ maintains in collaboration with the Quebec Justice Department, disseminates more than 300,000 legal and administrative decisions made in Quebec, free of charge.

3) Express newsletters: Weekly case-law summaries, including *Jurisprudence Express*, which covers all fields of law; *Droit du travail Express*, which covers labor laws, and other specialized newsletters produced every trimester.

4) Case-law reports: *Recueil de jurisprudence du Québec* (R.J.Q.), *Recueil en droit immobilier* (R.D.I.), *Recueil en droit de la famille* (R.D.F.), and others. These are summaries of jurisprudence, real estate law, and family law, respectively. While some full-text decisions reported are provided in the original English, the summaries and search tools (indexes, tables, Web interface, etc.) are in French.

THE PROJECT: STRATEGIC KNOWLEDGE MANAGEMENT (KM) TECHNOLOGY SELECTION

SOQUIJ is firmly positioned as a leader in the provision of legal information services. In the past few years, a number of new organizations were created who came into direct competition for the same clientele. As a result of this environmental change, the organization had to ensure that its reputation, brand, customer loyalty, and market leadership was not diminished in any way. One particular aspect of concern was maintaining technological leadership and innovation. SOQUIJ wanted to take steps to ensure that its team had access to the best possible tools in order to provide the best possible services in analyzing and disseminating legal information to its clients.

Project Description

The principal activity of SOQUIJ is to analyze and disseminate legal and administrative tribunal judgments to the legal community and business environment. The company offers access to more than 800,000 documents through its legal databases. SOQUIJ employs a fairly sophisticated indexing system and has organized legal content in a valid and pragmatic taxonomy structure. They also offer a value-added service to their clients in the form of jurisprudence summaries written up by experienced legal practitioners. These summaries represent a significant competitive advantage for SOQUIJ due to their consistently high quality and rigor.

It soon became clear, however, that the company could not manually summarize all legal content offered in their databases, as it is very labor-intensive and the already high volume of content will always continue to grow. As a result, a fairly significant portion of the texts available in their databases had not been summarized. In order to further increase the value of the services offered by their database, SOQUIJ wanted to explore the possibility of supplementing their manual summaries by using a knowledge management software tool that could automatically generate text summaries. In parallel, a number of competing organizations had begun using some automated taxonomy tools, primarily to provide contextual search capabilities. SOQUIJ therefore sought some recommendations on tools that could best meet their text summarization needs.

The recommended tool would be used in order to improve clients' access to legal content that was not yet available as summaries. The major tool selection criteria included easy and rapid summary production of the majority of unsummarized text available without adding additional work to the summary production team. The general approach was to find out whether other firms were using automated summarization software and if so, which ones, and to assess the quality of tools used with respect to the summaries produced. Four other legal information providers were analyzed using competitive intelligence (CI) techniques. Of these, two were found not to use any technology (manual text summarization only) while the other two used a prototype software from a university and the other a commercial tool called Delphes. A total of nine software tools were evaluated to assess how well they summarized legal texts. They included:

1. Inxight SmartDiscovery
2. CIRILab Instigator
3. Delphes—DioWeb
4. Pertinence Summarizer
5. EffectiveSoft—Intellexer Summarizer
6. Nstein—Nsummarize
7. Lextek—Brevity Document Summarizer8. Autonomy—Summarizer
9. Megaputer—TextAnalyst

Two others were eliminated from the project: Teragram—Summarizer due to the fact that a demo copy of the software could not be obtained despite repeated attempts and communications with the company; and LetSUM, which proved to be the object of a doctoral dissertation and was not available for evaluation or commercial purchase.

Return on Investment and Valuation Methods Used

Text summarization refers to a representing of the content of a document by a much shorter summary (typically 10 percent of the original length) containing only the salient points of the text. The primary goal of summarization is to make condensed representations of content aiding in information selection and indexing (Sparck Jones 1993).

The first attempts at automated text summarization were primarily driven by a desire to save time and effort, that is, to be able to know whether or not a given document contained the information readers were searching for (Salton et al. 1994). The same holds true today except that the volume of content has grown exponentially. The information overload that plagues all knowledge workers today means that text summarization has become a tool for the general population as well as for specialized information providers. "No one has time to read everything, yet we often have to make critical decisions based on what we are able to assimilate. The technology of automatic text summarization is becoming indispensable for dealing with this problem. Text summarization is the process of distilling the most important information from a source to produce an abridged version for a particular user or task" (Mani and Maybury 1999). In parallel, technological advances have made automated summarization more reliable and thus more interesting to implement in a variety of contexts (Minel 2004).

The major approach used in text summarization is "information extraction." Information extraction is about processing one or more documents in order to extract from them some information that is relevant to us and then generating a brand new text (or another structure, as for instance a template) containing exactly that precise relevant information (Roca 2001; Farzindar and Lapalme 2005; Hahn and Mani 2000). Summaries by extraction, that is, *extracts*, process one (or several) document(s), seen as a collection of sentences. Among such a collection they retrieve and give back those considered most relevant—or else those responding to certain criteria. In this case, the summary is a subset of the set of sentences of the original text.

Text extraction is based on a combination of statistical and linguistic algorithms that determine which text contains salient points. The following formula is used to place a value on text importance: the presence of "cue phrases" (that announce a plan, a method, e.g., "in conclusion"), and the presence of key words found in the title or first paragraph of the document (location in text). Key word frequency is calculated, and each word is assigned a score:

$$\text{Total score} = \text{location} + \text{cue phrase} + \text{key word} + \text{frequency}$$

The summary is then constructed from the list of selected phrases that had the highest scores. The summaries normally represent 5–15 percent of the original text size.

The criteria that were used in both the competitive intelligence and in the evaluation of automated summarization tools for SOQUIJ included the following:

- quality of the summaries—that is, coherence, sequencing of phrases, presence of anaphors (a word or phrase that refers to another that is not specified, e.g., "this then led to")
- ease with which summaries could be read (clear, makes sense)
- relevance (pertinent content, represents integral text well, no repeated content)

- type of algorithms used (e.g., semantic, linguistic, statistical)
- price
- the ability to add functions such as indexing, categorization, automatic taxonomy generation, thesaurus construction, and so on
- the quality of customer service offered

In addition to these criteria, a number of critical factors should be included in good summaries. These include:

- What is the subject of the litigation?
- What were the key legal decisions made?
- What was the result (e.g., judge's conclusion)?
- Which articles of law were applied?

A minimum of eight legal documents from the SOQUIJ database were used to assess the text summarization tools. The summaries were set at 10 percent each.

Delphes was a taxonomy software tool used by one of the legal information providers. Competitive analysis showed that the choice was made after a review of search engines that could perform natural language searches. The tool performed quite well and it allowed users to see the relevant parts of text to get a quick overview of the key content. These sections could be underlined, they could be extracted as key concepts, or they could be used to generate a text summary. However, the summaries were not found to be very relevant and it proved quite difficult to generate extracts related to litigation and decision contexts.

The second firm was found to be using a prototype software developed by a group of university researchers. The software tool consisted of ELIISA, an extraction and search engine and Reflex, a module used to identify and analyze legal references. The tool was bilingual and was able to analyze a large volume of legal information to be indexed. A summary text is produced with key words underlined. LetSUM is the automated summarizer module. LetSUM divides the original text into thematic sections based on key words and then filters the results to eliminate any nonrelevant sections. However, the major drawback of this software is that it is not commercially available or commercially supported.

An evaluation of KM tools was carried out using the same criteria as those for the CI tools. Based on the evaluation using the above criteria, three alternatives were recommended to assist SOQUIJ in its strategic decision making:

1. Nstein—offering complete summaries and, highly personalized customer service. In addition it was modular, and additional functions could be added easily. The price was high but competitive.

2. Megaputer TextAnalyst or CiriLabs Instigator—both use hybrid approaches that are similar to Delphes. The tool allows contextual navigation more than automated summarization.
3. Continue to explore and find other alternatives (e.g., partnership with a university research group).

WHAT ACTUALLY HAPPENED WITH THE PROJECT

The SOQUIJ team was not ready to immediately make a choice and requested that additional tools be assessed and that a recommendation be revisited. To this end, the project was extended and two more tools were evaluated, using the same texts and the same criteria: Nomino Technologies and Copernic Technologies.

Nomino Technologies is an excellent natural language search engine, but it does offer the same summarizer functions as the other tools. During a demonstration, 2,000 SOQUIJ documents were treated (representing several years' worth of legal content) and there was excellent key word extraction. This software is best suited for automated indexation and metadata generation but not text summarization. Other shortcomings include the absence of a thesaurus, the inability to treat numbers (each legal case has a unique identifier case number), and the necessity of creating a list of concepts beforehand. SOQUIJ already has a strong competency in indexation, and this software did not meet their text summarization needs.

Copernic Technologies performed quite well but only when the summary size was set at 50 percent. The performance was not as good at 10 percent, which is what is required for the SOQUIJ content to be summarized.

Other software that was looked at included those being used by law offices and other legal practitioners—namely, Zylab MetaTagger, Hummingbird Enterprise KM, and RealPractice ACE Profiler (Lamont 2006). MetaTagger provides an enterprise service for intelligently and automatically categorizing content and extracting information based on business requirements, organizational standards, taxonomies and collective knowledge. Hummingbird Enterprise KM provides a preview of documents via summaries to quickly determine relevance and pinpoints relevant information quickly through statistical relevance ranking, result-list clustering, and highlighting of search terms within documents in all supported formats.[2] RealPractice ACE Profiler allows the extraction of content specifically for law firm products using algorithms to discern the legal issues, jurisdictions, and document types pertaining to each discrete document in the collection. This information is collected in abstracts.[3]

These additional analyses refined the original three alternatives to provide the following recommendations:

1. Nstein—offered complete summaries, highly personalized customer service, was modular and additional functions could be added easily, the price was high but competitive.
2. Megaputer TextAnalyst or CiriLabs Instigator—both use hybrid approaches that are similar to Delphes, the tool allows contextual navigation more than automated summarization. Copernic Summarizer may also be used as a task support system to produce real-time summaries of search results and is also similar to the Delphes software.
3. Continue to explore and find other alternatives (e.g., partnership with a university research group or prototyping required modules with Nomino Technologies).

SOQUIJ felt the first alternative recommended, NSTEIN, held the most promise. The internal project team members had tested out the summaries produced by the various tools and were in agreement that NSTEIN produced superior quality summaries. The quality of the end product was in fact the most important criterion, as poor quality summaries would diminish the positive image SOQUIJ currently enjoys as the provider of value-added legal information services. Despite the high sticker price of the solution, which varies depending on the modules selected, the company felt that this product could provide an interesting avenue to investigate further.

To this end, NSTEIN's N-Summarizer was tested more thoroughly in a pilot project. The goal of the pilot project was to see whether or not the tool corresponded to SOQUIJ's business needs, namely, to decrease the cost of producing summaries and to increase the number of summaries produced, using some form of text summarization. The testing was carried out on a representative sample of judgments that are processed by SOQUIJ.

Labor law documents were well categorized by the tool, but the summary results were mixed. In certain cases, the summaries were quite clear and addressed the salient points, while in other cases the results were incomplete and/or lacked coherence. The pilot project also showed that the presummarization work of categorization was required in order to arrive at a better-targeted summary that resumed the key points well. Summaries produced using noncategorized documents were of a much-diminished quality.

On the other hand, when a taxonomy of legal terms was added to further help classify documents, and some of the software parameters were modified, N-Summarizer performed much better. The SOQUIJ team felt that if properly "tuned," N-Summarizer could indeed be used to decrease the time needed to produce certain types of summaries. The best approach would likely be to use the tool to produce a "first draft" summary, which could then be completed, corrected, and refined by the legal officer.

However, the general mind-set is that an automated tool can never replace the human knowledge organizer. The summaries that are generated cannot be directly made available online as is—some human editorial input, at the very least, will always be required. To this end, automated text summarizer tools can be used to provide a starting point that can then be manually optimized. A complementary or hybrid approach appears to be the best way to proceed, making use of the strengths of both humans and computers to create a synergistic improvement to productivity and quality results. In addition, SOQUIJ realized that the results of text summarization using N-Summarizer were enhanced if the N-Categorizer tool was used in conjunction with the summaries. The company is thus considering the implementation of these two modules in order to save time in producing good summaries that are well indexed, while maintaining the "human in the loop" at all times.

SUCCESSES AND FAILURES

The major failure was the inability to assess some of the software tools, due either to difficulty in obtaining demo or trial versions (as it was unreasonable to purchase such expensive tools solely to assess them) or due to the fact that they were prototypical tools resulting from university research labs (and thus, equally unavailable).

The major success was that the results of this comparative analysis allowed ȘOQUIJ to better understand the strengths and limitations of taxonomy tools and to then select the most promising one to investigate further.

EPILOGUE

> The person who is best informed is not the one with the most information but the one with the best means for obtaining and assimilating (consuming) exactly the information acquired. . . . In this context, automated document summary systems are a new step forward towards optimising the treatment of documentation in digital formats and for tailoring it to the needs of users.
>
> —Roca 2001, 1

The combination of competitive intelligence and knowledge management makes eminent sense, as there is a great deal of synergy in combining the conceptual approaches and the practical tools and techniques (Bouthillier and Dalkir, 2005). Knowledge management has a tendency to look inward and backward (relying heavily on lessons learned and reusing best practices generated internally). There is often a benchmarking component to KM, but this is rarely taken to the strategic decision-making level, which is the most valuable contribution of competitive intelligence. CI tends to look outside and to the future and has as a specific objective to provide valuable and relevant information to aid strategic decision making. An integrated KM and CI approach is therefore best suited to ensuring that strategic decisions are made with the best available information.

NOTES

Acknowledgments: The author would like to thank Daniel Champagne and Carole Piché-Burton for providing this opportunity to show how CI and KM can provide a complementary approach to such a challenging field and Stéphanie Lemieux, who carried out the comparative analyses of automated taxonomy software in a proficient and highly professional manner, deserves thanks as well.

1. From the SOQUIJ website, English Overview, available at: www.soquij.qc.ca/societe/english.html.
2. From www.hummingbird.com/products/enterprise/km/index.html?virtual_url_referrer=/products/km/feature.html.
3. From www.realpractice.com/about_rpace.html.

REFERENCES

Bouthillier, F., and K. Dalkir. 2005. "Knowledge Management and Competitive Intelligence: Examination of Similarities, Differences, and Intersections." In *Knowledge Management: Nurturing Culture Innovation and Technology. Proceedings of the 2005 International Conference on Knowledge Management*, ed. S. Hawamdeh, 603–10. Hackensack, NJ: World Scientific.

Farzindar, A., and G. Lapalme. 2005. "Production Automatique du Résumé de Textes Juridiques: Évaluation de Qualité et d'Acceptabilité. " *TALN 2005*, Dourdan, 6–10 juin.

Hahn, U., and I. Mani. 2000. "The Challenges of Automatic Summarization." *Computer* 33(11): 29–36.

Lamont, J. 2006. "KM for Law Firms—Legal or Not?" *KM World*, July/August, 2006. Available from www.kmworld.com/Articles/ReadArticle.aspx?ArticleID=16918.

Mani, I., and M. Maybury, eds. 1999. *Advances in Automatic Text Summarization*. Cambridge, MA: The MIT Press.

Minel, J-L. 2004. "Le Résumé Automatique de Textes: Solutions et Perspectives." *TALN*, 5(1):7–13.

Roca, S. 2001. "Automatic Text Summarization." *Digithum, Volume 3*. Available from www.uoc.edu/humfil/digithum/digithum3/catala/Art_Climent_uk/climent/climent.html.

Salton, G., J. Allan, C. Buckley, and A. Singhal. 1994. "Automatic Analysis, Theme Generation, and Summarization of Machine-readable Texts." *Science* 264:1421–26.

Sparck Jones, K. 1993. "What Might Be in a Summary?" In *Information Retrieval '93*, ed. G. Knorz, J. Krause, and C. Womser-Hacker, 9–26.

8

Knowledge Management and Value-Driven Healthcare

Rajeev Bali, Nilmini Wickramasinghe, and Steve Goldberg

The healthcare industry is facing tremendous pressure globally to significantly stem escalating costs and contemporaneously make dramatic improvements with regard to increasing the quality of delivery of healthcare. Many believe healthcare is facing a major crisis globally (National Coalition on Healthcare 2004; Pallarito 1996; European Institute of Medicine 2003; WHO 2000, 2004; Kyprianou 2005; Frost & Sullivan 2004; Plunkett Research 2005; OECD 2004; NCHS 2002; Russo 2000). The Chinese word for *crisis* is made up of two characters, the first meaning "challenge" the second meaning "opportunity." Both terms are most suitable to describe the current dynamics faced by healthcare professionals.

As technology continues to advance at an ever-increasing exponential rate, we evidence more and more possibilities for innovative applications of these technologies in the healthcare domain. The opportunities for technology-enabled devices, more effective pharmaceutical drugs, and new developments in minimally invasive diagnostic and surgical techniques represent the three primary areas for investment in research and development (R&D) in healthcare (Lacroix 1999; Lee et al. 2003; Blair 2004; Kulkarni and Nathanson 2005; Wickramasinghe, and Silvers 2003; Wickramasinghe and Mills 2001; von Lubitz and Wickramasinghe 2006). Ultimately, the challenge is to move from good idea to commercialization of the product so that the patient can be the ultimate beneficiary and the healthcare industry can address its current crisis. Integral to moving from idea to commercialization is the inclusion of value-added factors and the ensuring of return on investment (ROI). We illustrate the power of this approach with the example of the Wi-INET model for m-health, a knowledge-driven business-delivery model.

CASE DESCRIPTION

In 1998, INET International Inc. was founded by Steve Goldberg. INET is a Canadian-based information and communication technology (ICT) management firm. The company specializes in online data collection for international research studies, wireless healthcare programs, and annual INET mini-conferences. Through these areas of expertise INET delivers advanced online surveys for physician studies, develops and implements programs that support chronic disease management with a focus on diabetes, builds consensus on new ways to deliver healthcare, and leads the development of ICT best practices to support healthcare professionals.

Wi-INET Model for M-Health

Successful m-health (i.e., mobile communications and network technologies for healthcare systems) projects require a consideration of many components. Figure 8.1 provides an integrative model for all key factors that we have identified through our research that are necessary in order to achieve m-health excellence (Wickramasinghe et al. 2005; Goldberg et al. 2002a, 2002b, 2002c, 2002d, 2002e; Wickramasinghe and Goldberg 2004). What makes this model unique and most beneficial is its focus on enabling and supporting all areas necessary for the actualization of information and communication technology initiatives in healthcare. By design, since fundamentally this is a business model, the model identifies

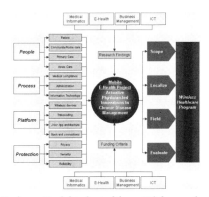

Figure 8.1. Wi-INET Business Model (adapted from Wickramasinghe and Goldberg 2004)

the inputs necessary to bring an innovative chronic disease management solution to market. These solutions are developed and implemented through a physician-led mobile e-health project. This project is the heart of the model to bridge the needs and requirements of many different players into a final output deliverable as a "Wireless Healthcare Program." To accomplish this, the model is continually updated to identify, select and prioritize the ICT project inputs that will:

a. Accelerate healthcare system enhancements and achieve rapid healthcare benefits. The model identifies the key healthcare system inputs with the "four Ps": (1) People that deliver healthcare, (2) Process to define the current healthcare delivery tasks, (3) Platform used in the healthcare technology infrastructure, and (4) Protection of patient data.
b. Close the timing gaps between information research studies and its application in healthcare operational settings.
c. Shorten the time cycle to fund an ICT project and receiving a return on the investment.

IT Architecture and Standard Mobile Environment

By adopting a mobile/wireless healthcare delivery solution it is possible to achieve rapid healthcare delivery improvements that impact both the costs and the quality of healthcare delivery. This is achieved by using an e-business acceleration project, which provides hospitals a way to achieve desired results within a standardized mobile Internet (wireless) environment. Integral to such an accelerated project is the ability to build on the existing infrastructure of the hospital. This then leads to what we call the three-tier web-based architecture.

In such an environment, tier one is essentially the presentation layer, which contains the web browser, but no patient data is stored within this layer, thereby ensuring compliance with international security standards/ policies such as the Health Insurance Portability and Accountability Act (HIPAA). Tier two is the HTTP server and basically provides the business logic, including but not limited to lab, radiology, and clinical transcription applications; messaging of HL7, XML, DICOM, and other data protocols; and interface engines to a Hospital Information Systems (HIS), Lab Information Systems (LIS), Radiology Information Systems (RIS), as well as external messaging systems such as Smart Systems for Health (an Ontario Healthcare IT infrastructure project). This latter messaging feature may also be included in third-tier back-end database servers like, Oracle, MySQL, or Sybase.

MAPPING CASE STUDY TO BUSINESS MODEL

During the past six years INET has used an e-business acceleration project to increase ICT project successes (Goldberg et al. 2002a, 2002b; 2002c, 2002d, 2002e; Wickramasinghe and Goldberg 2004). Today INET is repurposing the project into a mobile e-health project to apply, enhance, and validate the Wi-INET model. Such a model provides a robust structure and in turn serves to ensure excellence in the m-health initiative. INET's data provide the perfect opportunity to examine the components of our model (figure 8.1) as it is both rich and longitudinal in nature. In mapping the data and specific business case, we have drawn upon many well-recognized qualitative techniques, including conducting both structured and unstructured interviews, in depth archival analysis, and numerous site visits. Goldberg et al. (2002a, 2002b, 2002c, 2002d, 2002e) and Wickramasinghe and Goldberg (2004) capture and substantiate the findings discussed, while Kavale (1996), Boyatzis (1998) and Eisenhardt (1989) detail the importance and richness of the methodologies we have adopted in presenting the following findings. Key criteria were established from Standish Group International Inc. (1994), the Committee on Quality of Healthcare in America (2001), and *Canadian Healthcare Technology* (2005).

A necessary first step in developing the Wi-INET model was to ensure it meets the objectives of an INET mobile e-health project; this includes the following:

- Accelerate consensus building with an e-health solution that is focused on a disease state and driven by the medical model, with the primary objective to streamline communications and information exchange between patients and providers of community/home care, primary care, and acute care.
- Acquire commercial funding early with a compelling business case. For instance, enhancing therapeutic compliance can improve patient quality of life with significant healthcare cost savings. It is well documented that in diabetes this will have immediate and high-impact benefits for healthcare consumers, pharmaceutical firms, governments, insurers, and employers.
- Avoid risk by reengineering large-scale healthcare delivery processes in small manageable pieces. Today, organizations can harness a rigorous method to incrementally enhance a process one step at time. A way to achieve quick wins early and frequently.
- Rapid development of simple-to-use, low-cost, and private/secure information and communication technology solutions. Achieve these benefits through a wireless Application Service Provider (ASP). In

addition to rapid development, a wireless ASP can easily connect and bring together many independent healthcare information systems, and technology projects.

To enhance the delivery of mobile e-health projects, INET is looking to the Wi-INET model as an INET project engagement framework. For INET, this will support an INET mobile e-health project management office (PMO) to manage the costs and quality, deliver many small projects, and replicate projects for local and international distribution. As a first-case scenario to test the model, INET is proposing an INET wireless diabetes program with the leadership from a family physician. The INET PMO is provisioning a project manager to support this physician-led project to meet both research and commercial sponsors' interests and objectives in diabetes. INET uses a systems development life cycle (SDLC) approach to deliver these projects. An SDLC is a rigorous process of developing and deploying information and communication technology solutions through a multiple step process. For INET this includes a six-step delivery process:

- Roles and Responsibilities
- Investigation
- Analysis (Logical Design)
- Design (Physical Design)
- Implementation
- Maintenance

INET had trouble defining a standardize set of roles and responsibilities in healthcare to build the Wi-INET model and support the delivery of INET mobile e-health projects. After a number of failed attempts, INET skipped the first step to try and discover the roles and responsibilities with the results from the investigation step of the SDLC. This second step of SDLC involves the problem statement, solution, and business case and project definition. For an INET wireless diabetes program the investigation details are given below.

Problem Statement

There are many communication and information exchange bottlenecks between patients and their family physicians that prevent the effective treatment of diabetes. As background, a fundamental problem today is the ability to have a private and secure way to manage, search, and retrieve information at the point-of-care. In diabetes, physicians cannot quickly and easily respond to patients with high glucose levels. They need to wait for people to come to the office, respond to phone calls, reply using traditional mail delivery, or never receive the patient information.

Solution Mandate

Implement a diabetes monitoring program to enhance therapeutic compliance, such as a program to enhance the usage of oral hypoglycemic agents (drugs) and/or the usage of blood sugar monitoring devices. As background, everyone wins when enhancing patients' ability to follow instructions in taking prescribed medication. The patient's health, safety, and quality of life improve with significant healthcare cost savings. However, it is well documented that many patients do not stay on treatments prescribed by physicians.[1] This is where wireless technology may have the greatest impact to enhance compliance. One solution may be as simple as using a cell phone and installing a secure wireless application for patients to monitor glucose levels, and provisioning a physician to use a personal digital assistant (PDA) (connected to a wireless network) to confidentially access, evaluate and act on the patient's data.

Project Definition

Use an INET mobile e-health project to scope, localize, field, and evaluate an INET wireless diabetes program led by a physician. Each project can easily and simply customize a program to quickly meet the unique needs of a particular rural or urban healthcare delivery setting, age, ethnicity, income, language, and culture. These are small manageable projects. Each project collects data on patient–healthcare provider relationships, wireless medical informatics, therapeutic compliance business case, and ICT usability to accelerate acceptance of a wireless diabetes program using wireless technology. The program may include cellular network and application usage, support, healthcare provider PDA, and consulting fees for family physician and other healthcare providers. However it is expected that the costs may not include items such as consumer cell phone, medication, or blood sugar monitoring devices/supplies. It is recommended that commercial and/or research sponsor(s) pay for an INET project, and help subsidize the user costs.

THE BUSINESS CASE: RETURN ON INVESTMENT

Using Ontario Canada as an example, we have calculated that implementation of the Wi-INET system as an integral part of a wireless healthcare program to enhance patient care and safety may save a total of CAN$1,026,776,000 over three years. A key benefit is that patient's health and quality of life improves with significant cost savings. This may have the greatest impact on managing patients with chronic disease.

For instance, enhancing care for patients with diabetes in Ontario, Canada, may represent a cost savings of CAN$254,700,000. This has been calculated as follows:

TEXTBOX 8.1. ENHANCE PATIENT'S COMPLIANCE OF MEDICALLY PRESCRIBED TREATMENTS

Research has shown that intensive monitoring of people with diabetes can significantly reduce and/or delay the onset of complications.
This may save Ontarians approximately **CAN$254,700,000** as follows:

$$\$9,000,000,000 \times 38\% \times 2.5\% \times 3 \text{ years} =$$
the cost of mobile e-health projects

$9,000,000,000 = Canadian cost of diabetes per year
38% = Ontario's % national population
2.5% = potential benefit from enhancing communications and information flow between patients and healthcare providers

---

One way to achieve these healthcare benefits is to remove the communication and information bottlenecks between patients and healthcare providers. Many healthcare organizations are looking to portal technology. For instance, again in Ontario, Canada, this may represent a second cost savings of $450,120,000, calculated as follows:

TEXTBOX 8.2. REMOVE ADMINISTRATIVE TASKS FROM CLINICAL PROCESSES

Reduce the time to search, manage and access data by using wireless technology to support local and remote healthcare providers at the point of care, e.g., a mobile e-health project delivers a custom wireless application (PDAs) that accesses a portal to distribute, update, or access radiology reports, lab results, chart/case summaries, prescriptions, and/or patient diaries.
The portal may achieve administration cost savings of **CAN$450,120,000** as follows:

$$\$8,000 \text{ year} \times 18,755 \text{ physicians} \times 3 \text{ years}$$

Today, the pervasive availability of wireless devices and networks (PDAs and cell phones) can harness the benefit of a wired portal infrastructure. As a continuation of the Ontario example, this may represent additional savings of $321,956,000, calculated as follows:

TEXTBOX 8.3. LEVERAGE INVESTMENTS IN INFORMATION AND COMMUNICATION TECHNOLOGY

Avoid IT cost by augmenting a wired IT infrastructure with a private, secure and reliable wireless IT infrastructure. A case in point, the e-Physician Project (ePP), with wired costs of $150,000,000 for 6,400 family physicians plus Smart Systems for Health Agency (SSHA) $360,000,000 (estimated SSHA IT budget), can be enhanced with a low-cost wireless IT infrastructure.

If these programs implemented a wireless IT infrastructure the savings may total CAN$321,956,000:

One time hospital back-end data upgrade cost of $93,070,000 for
9 regions
×
2 hospitals/region
×
$5,000,000 and 207 [225 − 18] hospital sites
×
$10,000

Application server, messaging services, and wireless device (i.e., PDAs)
upgrade cost of $94,974,000 for
18,755 Ontario physicians, 14,561 community-based nurses
and 30,000 selected Ontarians with diabetes
×
$500/year/user
×
3 years
Total IT infrastructure cost savings is
($150,000,000 + $360,000,000)
−
(93,070,000 + 94,974,000)
=
$321,956,000

SUCCESSES AND FAILURES

After the investigation was completed, the roles and responsibilities were not well enough defined to engage an INET mobile e-health project. INET then proceeded to dive deeper into the SDLC by completing the next three steps: analysis, design, and implementation. The idea was to determine if the players involved in these steps could be applied to a general project engagement model.

In June 2005 INET continued to supply input for the Wi-INET model with the implementation of a wireless diabetes program. This was a pilot project, with the objective to decrease diabetes-related complications with better control of glycemic levels, measured by HA1c.

The core component of the program is the relationship between family physicians and patients supported by a wireless diabetes management protocol.[2] This protocol describes how a patient can enter their glucose readings into their cell phone and transmit the results to their family physician. The protocol further details how the physician, in turn, is able to monitor any number of patients on his PDA, such as a Palm Treo or RIM BlackBerry device. A physician, if required, can take immediate action with a message electronically sent to the patient's cell phone. The program was tested through a pilot project with four patients, led by Dr. Sheldon Silver, and was completed in July 2005. The pilot project lasted about three months. The preliminary results are significant, as shown in table 8.1.

EPILOGUE

In the current high-paced knowledge economy, commercialization of a good idea is important. Especially in healthcare, too many innovative ideas never make it to successful commercialization due to the inherent risks and lengthy development stages. The dynamic nature of the Wi-INET model facilitates the continuous incorporation of prior lessons and knowledge into the project process, thereby making it a truly knowledge-based methodology.

We have described the use of this methodology in the context of m-health initiatives. To be successful, wireless initiatives in healthcare require the coordination of many players. The Wi-INET business model and practice delivery framework ensure not only that all key elements are included but also that due consideration is given to technology, people, and process aspects of such initiatives. However, we note in closing that our case can be useful for all mobile initiatives and we urge for further application of the methodology in non-healthcare mobile initiatives.

Table 8.1. INET Wireless Diabetes Program Results

	INET Wireless Diabetes Program		
	Change in HA1c Levels		*Reduction in HA1c*
Patient	*Pre-Pilot*	*Post-Pilot*	
1	0.082	0.069	−.013
2	0.090	0.071	−.019
3	0.108	0.050	−0.58
4	0.113	0.084	−.029

NOTES

1. Fourteen to 21 percent of patients never fill their original prescription and 30 to 50 percent of patients ignore or otherwise compromise their medication instructions. Source: www.managedhealthcareexecutive.com/mhe/article/articleDetail.jsp?id=105388.

2. Wireless Diabetes Management Protocol © Dr. Sheldon Silver, MD 2005.

REFERENCES

Blair, J. 2004. "Assessing the Value of the Internet in Health Improvement." *Nursing Times* 100:28–30.

Boyatzis, R. 1998. *Transforming Qualitative Information: Thematic Analysis and Code Development*. Thousand Oaks, CA: Sage Publications.

Canadian Healthcare Technology. 2005. "Wireless reporting for diabetes patients offers up dramatic results." *Canadian Healthcare Technology* (September):4. Available from www.inet-international.com/INET/Update/PressCoverage2005.htm.

Committee on Quality of Healthcare in America. 2001. *Crossing the Quality Chasm: A New Health System for the 21st Century*. Washington, DC: National Academy Press, Institute of Medicine.

Eisenhardt, K. 1989. "Building Theories from Case Study Research." *Academy of Management Review* 14:532–50.

European Institute of Medicine. 2003. *Health Is Wealth: Strategic Vision for European Healthcare at the Beginning of the 21st Century*. Salzburg, Austria: European Academy of Arts and Sciences.

Frost & Sullivan. 2004. "Country Industry Forecast—European Union Healthcare Industry, May 11. Available from www.news-medical.net/print_article.asp?id=1405.

Goldberg, Steve, et al. 2002a. "Building the Evidence for a Standardized Mobile Internet (wireless) Environment in Ontario, Canada." January Update, internal INET documentation.

Goldberg, Steve, et al. 2002b. "HTA Presentational Selection and Aggregation Component Summary." Internal INET documentation.

Goldberg, Steve, et al. 2002c "Wireless POC Device Component Summary." Internal INET documentation.

Goldberg, Steve, et al. 2002d. "HTA Presentation Rendering Component Summary." Internal INET documentation.

Goldberg, Steve, et al. 2002e. "HTA Quality Assurance Component Summary." Internal INET documentation.

Kavale, S. 1996. *Interviews: An Introduction to Qualitative Research Interviewing.* Thousand Oaks, CA: Sage Publications.

Kulkarni, R., and L. A. Nathanson. 2005. "Medical Informatics in Medicine: E-Medicine." Available from www.emedicine.com/emerg/topic879.htm.

Kyprianou, Markos. 2005. *The New European Healthcare Agenda: The European Voice Conference "Healthcare: Is Europe Getting Better?"* Available from www.noticias .info/asp/aspcommunicados.asp?nid=45584.

Lacroix, A. 1999. "International Concerted Action on Collaboration in Telemedicine: G8 Sub-project 4." *Sted. Health Technol. Inform.* 64:12–9.

Lee, M. Y., S. A. Albright, T. Alkasab, D. A. Damassa, P. J. Wang, and E. K. Eaton. 2003. "Tufts Health Sciences Database: Lessons, Issues, and Opportunities." *Acad. Med.* 78:254–64.

National Coalition on Healthcare. 2004. *Building a Better Health: Specifications for Reform.* Washington DC: National Coalition on Healthcare.

NCHS (National Center for Health Statistics). 2002. *Health Expenditures 2002.* Hyattsville, MD: CDC/NCHS. Available from www.cdc.gov/nchs/fastats/hexpense.htm.

OECD (Organization for Economic Cooperation and Development). 2004. *OECD Health Data 2004.* CD-ROM (also available from www.oecd.org/health/healthdata).

Pallarito, K. 1996. "Virtual Healthcare." *Modern Healthcare* (March):42–44.

Plunkett Research, Ltd. 2004. *Plunkett's Health Care Industry Almanac, 2005 Edition.* Houston, TX: Plunkett Research, Ltd.

Russo, H. E. 2000. "The Internet: Building Knowledge and Offering Integrated Solutions to Health Care." *Caring* 19:18–31.

Standish Group International, Inc. 1994. *The CHAOS Report.* Available from www.standishgroup.com/sample_research/chaos_1994_1.php.

von Lubitz, D., and N. Wickramasinghe. 2006. "Healthcare and Technology: The Doctrine of Networkcentric Healthcare" *International Journal of Electronic Healthcare* 2 (4):322–44.

WHO (World Health Organization). 2000. *Health Systems: Improving Performance.* Geneva: World Health Organization.

WHO (World Health Organization). 2004. *Changing History.* Geneva: World Health Organization.

Wickramasinghe, N., and J. B. Silvers. 2003. "IS/IT The Prescription to Enable Medical Group Practices to Manage Managed Care" *Health Care Management Science* 6:75–86.

Wickramasinghe, N., and G. Mills. 2001. "MARS: The Electronic Medical Record System, the Core of the Kaiser Galaxy." *International Journal Healthcare Technology Management.* 3 (5–6): 406–23.

Wickramasinghe, N., et al. 2005. "Assessing E-health." In *E-Health Systems Diffusion and Use: The Innovation, The User and the User IT Model,* ed. T. Spil and R. Schuring. Hershey, PA: Idea Group Publishing.

Wickramasinghe, N., and S. Goldberg. 2004. "How M = EC2 in Healthcare." *International J. Mobile Communications* 2 (2): 140–56.

9

Utilizing Knowledge Management to Improve Patient Care

Avoiding Adverse Drug Reactions and Reducing Cost of Care through Clinical Pharmacy Productivity Measurement

Colleen Elliott and Joy Goldman

BACKGROUND ON THE HISTORY OF THE ORGANIZATION

Catholic Health Initiatives

Formed in 1996, Catholic Health Initiatives (CHI) is a national, non-profit health organization based in Denver, Colorado. CHI is the second-largest Catholic health system in the United States and the fifth-largest non-governmental health system in the United States (American Hospital Association 2005). CHI organizations offer acute-care, ambulatory care, long-term care and assisted-living services, residential facilities, and community-based health ministries. Leading product lines include orthopedics, cardiovascular, oncology, and gastroenterology. CHI consists of seventy-one hospitals; forty-two long-term care, assisted-living and residential facilities, and two community-based health ministries all located in nineteen states across the country (Catholic Health Initiatives n.d.). CHI employs 66,000 full- and part-time employees, had total assets of $9.6 billion in 2006, and had approximately 2 million acute, in-patient days in fiscal year ending 2005 (Catholic Health Initiatives 2006a).

Mission

The mission of CHI is to "nurture the healing ministry of the Church by bringing it new life, energy and viability in the 21st century." (Catholic

111

Health Initiatives 2006b, 9). Catholic Health Initiatives' vision is to live out its mission by transforming healthcare delivery and by creating new ministries for the promotion of healthy communities. In accomplishing this vision, CHI distinguishes itself by focusing on knowledge transfer that creates competitive advantage, and innovative partnerships with patients and their families, physicians, payers, and others that encourage and reward effective, new models of person-centered care. CHI has positioned information as a foundation to the success of all other strategic priorities.

Knowledge Management

The inherent value of CHI comes from leveraging the skills, expertise, and resources that associates bring to the healthcare facilities by transferring their skills, expertise, and resources across the organization. To facilitate effective knowledge transfer across the organization, CHI launched a knowledge management initiative in 2001. CHI leadership believed that identifying "pockets" of knowledge and leading practices, enabling the effective exchange of these practices, and then translating them into locally relevant solutions would result in sustainable performance improvement. Today, CHI has a comprehensive knowledge transfer and learning program that facilitates the effective spread of both successes and lessons learned across its facilities. The program includes knowledge communities, a database of proven and leading practices, an approach and tools for effective formal education and training, collaboration and communication tools, and consulting for how knowledge transfer and learning can advance strategic priorities.

The knowledge management team is part of the Strategy and Business Development Group, which positions the department as an integrated resource for achieving strategic goals. Because it is part of the Strategy Group within CHI, the knowledge management team has the ability to align its resources with strategic priorities and position its program as a critical method for achieving results. This helps to make knowledge transfer and learning explicit in *how* CHI goes about reaching its goals, so that sharing expertise and learning from others becomes the expected way the employees work together. Among CHI's strategic priorities are improving the quality of care and services and improving patient safety across the organization. One example of how knowledge transfer and learning contribute to these goals is through the pharmacy knowledge community.

PROJECT AND CASE DESCRIPTION

Pharmacy Services and Clinical Pharmacy Productivity Systems

Challenges facing CHI facilities include the complexity around providing the right drugs to the right patients at the right time, in the most cost-effective way. According to Classen et al. (1997), over 770,000 patients are injured or die each year from adverse drug events (ADEs) in the United States, and costs of treating these patients is estimated at $1.6 to $5.6 billion each year. ADEs also extend the length of stay for a hospitalized patient from one to five days, and double the likelihood of patient mortality (Classen et al., 1997).

Traditional pharmacy productivity measurement systems commonly utilized by hospital finance and performance management officers focus on drug distribution and fail to adequately evaluate patient-focused clinical pharmaceutical services. Unfortunately, pharmacist involvement in direct patient care, when a pharmacist intervenes to prevent adverse drug events (ADEs) and/or improve patient outcomes, has not traditionally been effectively tracked in pharmacy productivity measurements. This is mainly attributed to the lack of standardized methods by which to measure effectiveness. "Measuring what pharmacists do with their minds demonstrates and justifies the need for pharmacists at the patient bedside to improve care and reduce overall costs," emphasizes Tricia Killingsworth, R.Ph., national manager of pharmacy services at Catholic Health Initiatives (CHI). "The one single thing hospitals can do to improve patient care and reduce costs is to have pharmacists available at the patient's bedside to catch errors and optimize medication therapy regimes." Total productivity of clinical pharmacy departments is difficult to accurately benchmark and forces justification of patient-centered activities within cost-conscious healthcare organizations.

Clinical pharmacy leaders at CHI identified the need for a standardized clinical pharmacy productivity-measurement system to establish credibility of clinical pharmaceutical services with hospital finance and performance-management officers and to promote quality care and patient safety. In October 2003, a new knowledge community of clinical pharmacists focused on addressing this challenge through an integrated effort between the departments of pharmacy, decision support, and quality improvement. A Clinical Measurement Task Force was established with a charge to evaluate institution-specific measurement systems, review the medical literature, and develop an integrated clinical pharmacy productivity-measurement system that could be used nationally by CHI hospitals of varying size and clinical resources.

The Pharmacy Knowledge Community (PKC), a CHI community of practice that collaborates to develop and spread innovative solutions, facilitated this systemwide collaborative effort. The PKC has been working together since the 1980s and currently has more than 140 members. George Hill, R.Ph., national director of pharmacy services for CHI and leader of the Pharmacy Knowledge Community, describes the value of this community. "As a healthcare organization, it is critical that we have input from our employees who are involved with taking care of our patients directly when we shape our quality-improvement programs. Their direction and feedback helps us to develop the best, most viable programs, and ensures successful implementation. The knowledge community provides structure and opportunity for communication between the pharmacists and the system, and also provides an organized way to act on ideas and shared successes that bubble up through the community."

RETURN-ON-INVESTMENT VALUATION METHODS USED

Clinical Pharmacy Productivity-Measurement System (CPPMS) Results

As a result of this systemwide collaborative effort, a Clinical Pharmacy Productivity-Measurement System (CPPMS) was created and implemented at CHI. As figures 9.1 and 9.2 illustrate, between July 2004 and March 2005, nineteen hospitals expanded their clinical pharmacy activities, resulting in a cumulative financial impact of over $9 million (Jennings et al. 2005).

In addition, as illustrated in figure 9.3, avoidance of adverse drug events (ADEs) was the single largest activity that resulted in the greatest savings. Other interventions included anticoagulation measurement, pharmacokinetic and pain consults, and dose adjustments (figure 9.4).

As of December 2006, forty market-based organizations (MBOs) across the country have implemented the CPPMS. The system has now tracked 652,493 clinical pharmacy interventions with a combined value of $64 million and 199,796 man-hours (P. Killingsworth, personal communication, April 17, 2007).

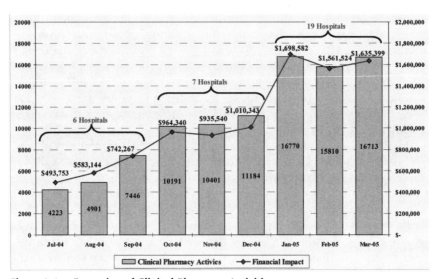

Figure 9.1.   Expansion of Clinical Pharmacy Activities

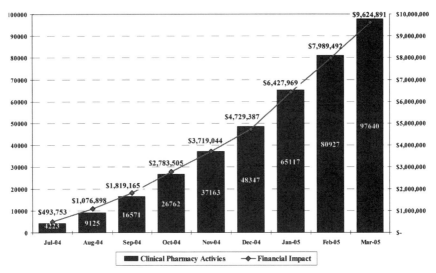

Figure 9.2.   Cumulative Impact of Integrated Clinical Productivity Tool

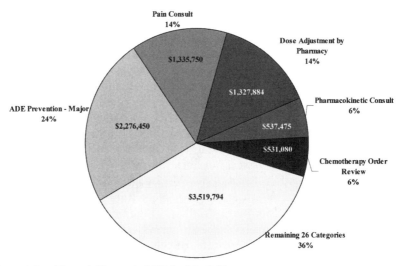

Figure 9.3.   Financial Impact of Clinical Activities

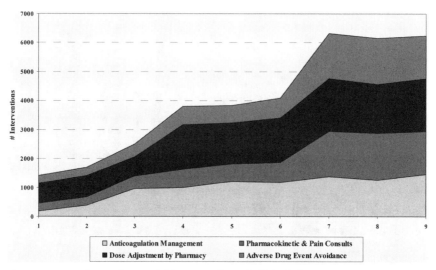

Figure 9.4.   Patient Safety Activities—Number of Clinical Pharmacy Interventions

WHAT ACTUALLY HAPPENED WITH THE PROJECT

Clinical Pharmacy Productivity-Measurement System

Members of the Clinical PKC began the program by identifying four critical areas of opportunity for improvement: standardized definitions of clinical services and interventions, standardized values used for time allocations associated with each service/intervention, standardized dollar values used for calculating financial impact to the institution, and evaluation of interventions to identify potential areas for improvement in patient healthcare (Jennings et al. 2005). Three large healthcare institution–specific pharmacy productivity-measurement systems were compared with the medical literature and combined to create an integrated productivity-measurement template. The PKC collaborated with the Decision-Support Knowledge Community and national finance staff to derive conservative values for financial impact and pharmacist time consumption of clinical pharmacy services. As a pilot, two MBOs began testing the integrated system in July 2004 and combined to document over 15,000 interventions and $2 million in savings during the initial four months. Education materials were developed to orient pharmacists, hospital leadership, and other key stakeholders to the implementation, utility, and value of the new system. The possibility then became a successful reality, and CHI has now implemented the program in 95 percent of its facilities.

The ability of the pharmacists to connect directly with the decision-support resources made it easier to develop a measurement standard consistent with other CHI measurement tools. It was also helpful to collaborate with a resource that could speak the same language as the health facility chief financial officers (CFOs) and facilitate buy-in for the value of this new measurement system. The fact that these knowledge communities exist as an entity made it easier to connect, as well as provided a recognizable, collective voice for these resources across CHI. This collective voice attracted more attention and gained more credibility with influential leaders.

Knowledge Communities and Collaboration

A key component to the success of the PKC and the Pharmacy Clinical Interventions initiative is the trust and collaborative relationships established between community members. These relationships foster creativity, sharing, and a unified sense of working together to advance what is best for the entire system. It also makes it easier for people to share both successes *and* mistakes. "Admitting to imperfections leaves the door open for discussions where we can learn from each others' mistakes and improve things," says Hill. Hill believes that getting to know each other both personally and professionally creates an environment where this type of sharing is safe. To foster this environment, the PKC meets in-person annually, and regions meet in-person on, at least, a quarterly basis. These networking opportunities make it easier for people to pick up the phone and make a call, or send an email, when facing a specific challenge. Regularly scheduled Clinical Pharmacy KC conference calls made it easier to answer questions and obtain feedback on the Clinical Interventions program.

The PKC also uses additional knowledge-transfer and learning tools to accelerate best-practice sharing in this trusted environment. An online collaboration space (see figures 9.5 and 9.5a) is utilized to organize and share critical information to advance their initiatives and decrease duplication of effort.

This collaboration space provides a centralized place for shared document repositories, calendars, discussion boards, and links to relevant online resources. The technology allows community members to "subscribe" to different components of the site, such as document folders or discussions, so that they are notified when new content is posted. The PKC actively utilizes the discussion board feature to track discussions and critical information, such as details on system wide contracting and program updates. "The collaboration tools have provided great value in connecting people across space and time to their peers, providing near real-time support and expertise," says Holly Pendleton, manager of Knowledge Management, who is the knowledge management team member responsible for supporting the knowledge transfer and learning needs of the PKC.

Figure 9.5 & 9.5a.   Pharmacy Knowledge Community Collaboration Site

The PKC has also utilized a knowledge-transfer and learning program called "Idea Jam," a time-bound event where participants submit ideas on a specific topic to a discussion board and build from other participants' ideas and suggestions. The PKC successfully utilized this tool to obtain input from community members on the Medication Safety Plan, which is critical to insure that the plans and ideas are realistic and make sense to those who will implement the plan. Tools like the Idea Jam make it possible to quickly obtain comprehensive feedback across a geographically diverse organization, when face-to-face communication can be difficult.

Leadership and Recognition

In order to integrate knowledge transfer and learning into the way the organization works, it is important to recognize those who share their knowledge and experiences and adopt the best practices of others. Hill, Killingsworth, and the knowledge management team make concentrated efforts to recognize the work of the PKC and the individuals within the community. Each year at the PKC annual meeting, an awards ceremony is conducted and individual community members are recognized for their contribution to improving patient safety, quality of care, and the success of the PKC. In addition, community success stories are published across the organization via CHI's intranet and the knowledge transfer and learning "Relay Report" (see figure 9.6) in order to recognize the pharmacists' work and promote support and adoption of their programs.

The knowledge management team also provides Knowledge Community Health Reports (figure 9.7) to assist knowledge community leaders in cultivating their communities.

These reports provide statistics on community activities such as participation levels, most active participants, most frequently utilized materials, etc. The reports make it easier for the leaders to recognize star community members, as well as determine where they may need to focus to reenergize a community.

SUCCESSES AND KEY LEARNINGS

CHI's Pharmacy Knowledge Community demonstrates the incredible value that a focused effort on knowledge transfer and learning can provide an organization. In addition to the value it provides through the real dollar savings and demonstrated, significant patient-safety improvement, it also is an excellent example of what is possible when discipline and effort are applied toward creating an environment where sharing and learning is expected behavior. The knowledge transfer and learning program at CHI has developed

Figure 9.6.   CHI Relay Report

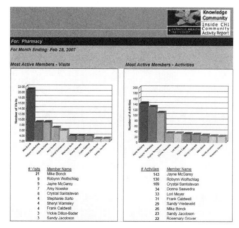

Figure 9.7.   Pharmacy Knowledge Community Health Report

in response to needs identified to support the PKC and to spread this discipline across the organization.

The implementation of a standard clinical-productivity system has increased pharmacist awareness of target clinical activities and elevated the level of clinical pharmacy practice throughout CHI. This assists pharmacists in key discussions about staff reductions and provides them with evidence to justify staffing levels. One key learning for the PKC was the recognition that some pharmacy leaders could benefit from development opportunities to improve their ability to communicate with senior leaders in the organization. The pharmacists need to be comfortable articulating key messages directly with senior leadership in order to maintain support. The PKC has added leadership development as an initiative to their strategic plan, in order to address this challenge.

Another key learning is the length of time that it can take to promote new tools and new technology into existing communication patterns. Over the years, the PKC has evolved from phone calls and faxes to online collaboration spaces and web-conferencing tools. Taking the time to teach the effective use of these tools and continuously reinforce their use is important to help people change their habits. Providing a variety of methods for this reinforcement is also important, from demonstrations to instructor-led training to one-on-one sessions with individuals in front of their own computer.

EPILOGUE

CHI knowledge communities have grown to a total of thirty-four distinct communities. These range from clinically focused communities to those dealing with organizational change and learning. One of these, the CHI Change Agent Knowledge Community, consists of employees throughout CHI who are actively involved in facilitating change in their departments and organizations. Another, the CHI Learning Network, consists of professionals who share a passion and commitment for education and training activities that are targeted at enabling and supporting employee skills, competencies, and training requirements. Belonging to both of these knowledge communities helps employees to facilitate change within their hospital in a more effective way, and bring to market regulatory-compliant and comprehensive learning offerings at a far lesser cost than if they had to start from scratch. The online collaboration space for the Learning Network contains a repository of 100 shared education courses and an active discussion board where members regularly reach out to each other for help.

The KM team has grown in size from one individual in 2001, to six employees, including a director, three managers, a learning analyst, and a project coordinator. In addition to supporting the cultivation of the thirty-four knowledge communities, a collection of clinically and organizationally aligned proven practices are published and available across CHI. The team has created standards for developing and implementing education programs, and is in the process of implementing a systemwide learning management system to enhance the ability to disseminate and track successful programs. Now that the infrastructure of the knowledge-transfer and learning program is created, a key role for the team is to advance the awareness of these resources and provide direct consulting for their utilization in advancing strategic priorities. The KM team utilizes CHI's intranet, the Relay Report, and internal strategic consulting projects to continuously provide awareness of the wealth of experience and successes that exist within the organization and connect people to these resources.

REFERENCES

American Hospital Association. 2005. *AHA Annual Survey*. Chicago: American Hospital Association.

Catholic Health Initiatives. n.d. CHI general information. Available from http://home.catholichealth.net/portal/site/chihome/menuitem.c0e5676baa1712 9f579df0ef43abafa0/?vgnextoid=385838d38bfab010VgnVCM10000026bcfa0aR CRD (retrieved April 11, 2007).

Catholic Health Initiatives. 2004. "Comprehensive Healthcare Environmental Assessment." Available from https://home.catholichealth.net/static-vcm/Inside%20CHI/ CHI%20General/Documentation/2004%20Final%20EA-05-01-04.pdf (retrieved March 25, 2007).

Catholic Health Initiatives. 2006a. *Journey Together: 2006 Annual Report*. Available from http://www.catholichealth.net/documents_public/Annual%20Reports/2006AR.pdf (retrieved March 25, 2007).

Catholic Health Initiatives. 2006b. *Catholic Health Initiatives 2007–2011 Strategic Plan.*, Available from https://home.catholichealth.net/static-vcm/Inside%20CHI/ Communications/Quick%20Reference%20(home%20page)/INSIDE%20CHI%2 0-%20Update%20of%20Strategic%20Plan%20Approved%20in%20July %202006.pdf (retrieved March 25, 2007).

Catholic Health Initiatives. 2007. "FY 07 Q2 12-31-06" CHI reporting group disclosure. Available from http://catholichealthinitiatives.com/documents/Financial _Information/F.%20FY07Q2%2012%2D31%2D06%20CHI%20Reporting%20Gr oup%20disclosure.pdf (retrieved March 25, 2007).

Classen, D. C., S. L. Pestonik, R. S. Evans, J. F. Lloyd, and J. P. Burke. 1997. "Adverse Drug Events in Hospitalized Patients: Excess Length of Stay, Extra Costs, and Attributable Mortality. *Journal of the American Medical Association* 277 (4): 301–6.

Jennings, H., K. Martin, H. Shaban, M. Wilson, T. Killingsworth, and G. Hill. 2005. "Development, Implementation, and Impact of a Standardized Clinical Pharmacy Productivity Measurement System." Poster session presented at the American College of Clinical Pharmacists (ACCP) Conference, Myrtle Beach, South Carolina, April.

10

A Bottom-Up Strategy for a KM Program Implementation at EDC

Eduardo Rodriguez

This case is a description of the different concepts and steps used in the development of knowledge management (KM) at Export Development Canada (EDC). The document is divided into three main sections: first, EDC in the business environment; second, the KM journey at EDC; and third, the basis of the KM project.

EDC IN THE BUSINESS ENVIRONMENT

EDC is a Crown Corporation that provides financing and risk management services to Canadian exporters and investors in up to 200 markets worldwide. EDC reports to the Canadian Parliament through the minister of international trade.

In 2006 EDC's services and deal-structuring capabilities helped to facilitate $66 billion in transactions for nearly 7,000 Canadian companies. Approximately 90 percent of EDC's customers are small and medium-size businesses. Canadian companies utilize EDC services in virtually every world market; however, those services can be particularly effective in facilitating trade and investment in emerging markets that are opportunity rich but that can also pose increased levels of risk.

EDC's mandate is to support and develop Canada's export trade and Canadian capacity to engage in that trade and to respond to international business opportunities. To fulfill this mandate, EDC provides trade finance and risk mitigation services to Canadian companies involved in export trade. EDC products and services complement the programs and services of commercial banks.

The business can be described in general as a support to Canadian exporters through credit insurance, political risk insurance, financing, equity services, bonding services, and guarantee services. EDC provides export credit insurance to protect against uncontrollable events such as a buyer refusing to pay. The organization adapts the services depending on the customer's attributes, economic sectors, distribution channels, and the need of tailored products.

EDC operates like a business, collecting interest on loans and premiums for the insurance. This allows the organization to be financially self-sufficient, in contrast to other ECAs (export credit agencies) that rely on government subsidies.

THE KM JOURNEY AT EDC

A general view of the business presented in the previous section shows the knowledge need of many different variables and factors affecting country, sector, and buyer risks, all of which can modify the exporter's capacity and the feasibility of international trade. EDC is a knowledge-intensive business, comprising core activities of underwriting, lending, and risk-management decisions, having a trusted advisory role with a significant proprietary automation with a very wide scope.

According to Nonaka and Takeuchi (1995), knowledge can be classified as explicit or tacit. This classification was used at EDC in the design of the knowledge management (KM) plan and tools. The decision for setting the project up was to work with explicit knowledge and to introduce, in the next stages, the support to manage tacit knowledge. Therefore, the first question to ask was What is knowledge in this business? From the idea that knowledge is created every time that a new risk is identified (Shaw 2005), EDC is creating knowledge every time there is a transaction. Therefore, the KM processes can be associated with each business-risk process and each kind of risk inside the organization. Risk knowledge can be expressed in examples, as shown in textbox 10.1. These examples represent a clear relationship to the decision-making process.

However, in addition to knowledge identification there are more strategic considerations that can affect the proper use of knowledge assets, such as staff retirement, prevalence of silos of knowledge on interdisciplinary work; lack of customer and user-centric point of view of the business; and reduced capacity to offer expertise as a service to the exporters, markets, sectors, and companies. Table 10.1 summarizes the main points to be taken

---

TEXTBOX 10.1. RISK ANALYSIS AND DECISION-MAKING PROCESSES

Risk Analysis
- Risk assessment
- Problem solving
- Business intelligence
- Exporter relationships
- Market knowledge
- Risk-mitigation knowledge
- Risk-modeling process
- Technical advisory and sector knowledge
- Interpreting risk ratings
- Risk classification in different fields

Decision-Making Processes
- Prediction of potential events that can change the financial results
- Development of a program in the financing world or in IT
- Building documents with a new concept or suggestion or judgment or recommendations
- Providing new concepts, suggestions, judgments and recommendations for transactions
- Passing from symptoms to diagnostics in evaluation of opportunities and transaction
- Development of proposals and business solutions

---

into consideration in the KM implementation. These points were identified in interviews with the organization's members using the KM processes proposed by Alavi and Leidner (2001) of knowledge creation, knowledge storage and retrieval, knowledge transfer, and knowledge application.

EDC's previous experience in fields or initiatives related to KM was based on the above interviewees' comments. These initiatives were not called KM, and their life spans have varied. Some of them are no longer in place, for others the use has been very limited, and some others have gained a wider development. The initiatives can be related to the four KM processes as follows:

- Knowledge creation: Interdisciplinary groups, innovation initiative, data mining
- Storage/retrieval: data warehousing, case data storage
- Transfer: interdisciplinary groups, information center, intranet, document management, learning and development
- Application: expertise locator, data feeds, cross-selling, reporting

Additionally, there are multiple applications that could be related and coordinated in order to support a more efficient and effective decision-making process, for example, applications of the operation-transaction of the business, human resources, business development, marketing, web channel, and others.

Table 10.1. Employee's Point of View with Regard to the KM Processes

Concept	Main Points and Issues Identified by the Employees Influencing a KM Application (Different Areas and Roles)
Organization	• Emphasis on transactions and not on customers. No centralized view of the customer. • Evident mismatch between content and tools in some cases. The process can be considered an inhibitor and not technology for knowledge sharing. • Services are not talking to one another. Lack of communication. • Differentiation of the expertise from other organizations, how the customer can distinguish the organization from others that have some similarities. • Missing links among communities of practice, knowledge products, interactions, and creation and delivery of solutions.
Knowledge description	• No clear concept of knowledge to use inside the organization. There are different understandings. • Time spent on interpreting information or creating knowledge. • Orientation of the business to risk control and support. • The value creation through knowledge is not clear. • The need to know an Inventory of knowledge types and sources. • Knowledge is at the center of EDC's business, but it is not part of the business strategy, yet.
Web channel / intranet	• Department/team focus on the intranet and on the user. • Independence of publishing and variety of content and methodologies to complete the area presentation. What is the connection to different content? • Updating process and value of search engine is questionable. • A lot of information on how to select. Need of filters.
Knowledge creation	• There is no time and capacity for experimentation. • Specialization introduces a limitation because everything depends on the individuals only. • There is no systematic methodology to create knowledge; it is reactive.
Knowledge transfer	• Culture of silos. • No communities of practice or problem solving. • Low follow-up to knowledge sharing, and there is no systematic plan for sharing knowledge. • Knowledge sharing in a team is more difficult than outside the team. • There are categories of knowledge to share. Technical and specific subjects are easier to share.
Knowledge store / retrieve	• There is not good documentation; a lot of tacit knowledge is potentially lost. • Reinventing the wheel is common; there is overlap of projects. • Unusual transactions are documented only with a memorandum, and the applications do not have the functionality for good documentation. • Different people can have different methods of analysis and interpretation. The analysis depends on the amount of information available • There is no answer to: How is the company keeping the knowledge?
Knowledge application	• Knowledge should have priorities for using it: dealing with bankers/transactions, operation/reporting.

People's ideas and previous experience with KM have been the input for the KM project, organizing and prioritizing the project and the knowledge management system (KMS) design. This input can be summarized as the search for a KM project that looks for business answers and solutions such as:

- Manage explicit knowledge transfer in order to support business activities and transactions
- Increase of business volume through increasing cross-selling, improving customer orientation, and developing country and sector-cluster analysis
- Reduce costs: less repetition and more coordination
- Improve satisfaction index: internal-external improvement, the customer can have an integral view
- Improve efficiency and cost reduction of the processes: processes coordination and development through knowledge sharing
- Enhance productivity improvement: a result of process improvement and knowledge sharing, allowing the distribution channels of knowledge for internal and external customer to improve.
- Improve innovation through new solutions that are potentially new services
- Reduce the abundance of information—more focus on quality than on quantity of data
- Organize, categorize, and identify the information and knowledge silos that can be shared and analyzed from marketing research, from external sources, from lessons learned of the market developers and many other sources
- Support the relationships between knowledge issuers and users

Thus, taking into consideration the above purposes and experiences and the search for applications of knowledge in the business practice, the KM program attributes were defined. They are described in the following sections.

THE BASIS OF THE KM PROJECT

The program is based on a bottom-up approach, with the purpose of achieving: first, the basis for a common language about KM; second, the ability to analyze the knowledge management strategy and act based on that strategy; third, the capacity to make investment decisions with regard to the knowledge management strategy.

The knowledge concepts presented in textbox 10.1 are the basis for connecting users with suppliers of risk knowledge. For example, the country knowledge can be linked to economic, political, and social knowledge and at the same time be related and tied to all kinds of risk exposure of the organization: operational, financial, strategic, physical, and marketing. Currently, country knowledge resides in multiple locations, with different people involved, data marts, data warehouse files, intranet files, Internet, credit agencies, and so on. In some cases, there is a duplication of information and conflicting messages; the effort to locate and extract information and knowledge is significant; the information format is not easily accessible; and the information is not always kept up-to-date and is not always tied to achieving the company's objectives and to supporting several areas and business drivers.

The KM processes (Alabi and Leidner 2001; Warren, 2002) in the KM program are seen as the means to consolidate, integrate, and organize knowledge. For instance, creation of knowledge is represented by risk assessment; storage and retrieval is part of the data support for external and internal users; transfer is the use of experience of many people about known cases; and application is seen as the discovery of opportunities for guiding customers and connecting people, processes, and technology.

Guiding Principles

The KM concepts, from textbox 10.1, and the organization's needs presented in table 10.1 are the sources of the principles to guide the KM plan. The guiding principles are build by blocks a positive mind-set about KM in order to achieve the creation of a general policy and wider involvement of areas; look for initiatives with business orientation; find applications to an area where the problems can widely affect the operation; find sponsors; provide good communication and a clear map of next steps; develop coordination with the other areas and an educational process in parallel to implementation; and finally, identify solutions, including the main three factors: business processes, software, and a clear responsibility of benefit realization.

Based on the guiding principles, the steps for implementation were prioritized in the KM program as follows: first, consolidation of country and sector information because countries and sectors are where the risks reside and where the exposure increases; second, filtering and simplifying the search based on the user's needs; third, sharing knowledge from different areas; fourth, supporting commercialization and the decision-making process; fifth, allowing a unified view across the organization, and sixth, supporting of users who are in the first line of contact with customers.

Remarks and Practice in the KM Project Development

The KM project and the KMS relationship are described in this section. The steps have been summarized and related to the conception of a KMS based on the four pillars represented by alignment, integration, connection, and coordination of the efforts for creating a real application of KM processes to the development of business processes. Alignment is represented by the balanced interaction of the components of the KMS infrastructure and the consolidation of knowledge to answer the customer's needs according to different segments. The concept of integration is related to the application of KM processes to the business processes in a company division or for the organization as a whole. This integration is preserving the strategy and the processes of preselling, selling, and postselling products and services of the organization. Connection and coordination are the creation of links between knowledge issuers and kinds of knowledge that have been required for solving transactions or customers' questions through a KMS.

The KMS design is related to business processes, and the purpose is to take actions connecting KM processes with business processes. The following are examples of actions taken:

- Focusing on a KM strategy that mobilizes EDC's knowledge transfer to the exporters using the web channel
- Bringing in experts and practitioners to talk about their KM experiences
- Implementing a cluster of explicit knowledge for countries (called country portal)
- Participating in other projects to coordinate efforts such as business intelligence, connectivity of international operation, and sector portal
- Developing prototypes for the KM strategy based on international business in order to solve the knowledge needs on the exporter's value chain
- Developing portal strategy and portal solutions for specific audiences of bankers, brokers, and customers, and ultimately providing online transaction support to them

The connection of business processes with KM processes ideally provides capability; flexibility; access; real time to the operation; and the means for collecting, sharing, and distributing knowledge. The access to knowledge is conceived through a user-friendly interface that is available with portals technology. The consolidated knowledge should include, in the first stage, explicit knowledge from documents and reports; and in the next stages virtual work, data feed, capture of the experience with cases, external knowledge of the markets, and many other tools supporting decision-making processes.

Finally, the concept of a bottom-up approach is an option that has budget benefits in two main ways: First, it is possible to use the initiatives and projects that are related to KM and the KMS design. For example, the business intelligence infrastructure is already in place and it is not directly cost related to the KM project. The portal infrastructure that is required for supporting the KMS is considered independent of the KM project because it is the answer to other projects and business processes already in place. Second, the direct cost of the KM project is not high. It has been close to CAN$300,000, just enough to cover the requests and development of a basic KM structure.

The downside of the bottom-up approach is the management of the indirect costs, given the independent developments of the projects related to KM. The reason for taking care of indirect costs is that the cost can grow given duplication of efforts and in some cases duplication of tools used in order to produce results in the business processes.

In order to illustrate the steps of implementation, the next section presents some examples in the KM project that build some of the required blocks, including the portal concept as a knowledge-delivery solution.

Examples of KM Work

The first example is the country knowledge tool (called internally country portal) and its lessons learned. The country knowledge tool is a good example of bottom-up strategy. This means content selection that takes into consideration identification and selection of the explicit knowledge for customer contact, based on the needs expressed by the users. The users are looking for a reduction in their time spent searching for answers, and this is based on their experience.

The most important experiences gained with the country knowledge tool design and ones that can be replicated in designing other blocks of the KM project are the following:

- Review of contradictions of document content, similar content from different authors, no updating process, different messages
- Standardization of the content, reports, data, and information structures in order to share content and to get consistent results
- Increment of capacity to provide independent answers to different knowledge consumers or to create undifferentiated solutions
- Inclusion of attributes of the business processes related to people's expertise in order to select people using an expertise locator
- Review of the value of the documents from the users perspective
- Adjustment of document formats and presentations for identification and extraction of pieces and sections of those documents fundamentally for sharing
- Structuring of naming conventions and taxonomy for storing and retrieving documents

- Ungrouping of some knowledge that is part of the same document and is required independently
- Creation of links among different pages in order to find the correct document
- Changing of the practice of users and issuers to understand that knowledge is based on the capacity to share it
- Organization of data in order to give access to different software
- Production of content in two different languages
- Creation of prototypes for the definition of solutions and for communication with the programming group.

The experience in the process of designing and developing of the country knowledge tool produced some main benefits to the business: first, creation of business capacity through organized knowledge, improvement in multidisciplinary work, and development of the learning processes; second, introduction of a block of a KMS design providing tools for communication, data management, use of lessons learned, judgment, and other applications to risk assessment; third, creation of a methodology represented in experiences, practices, relationships, limitations, methods, opportunities, and barriers to perform the actions in risk-management implementation.

The second example is a proposed value chain KM model of the exporter. This model represents the basis for guiding future development of the KM strategy. This is the concept of the general KM strategy to build by blocks, using the concept of the exporter's value chain to fill the knowledge missing in the processes. The purpose is to find the proper ways to achieve solutions and answers in the knowledge gaps found. This view includes internal and external knowledge in order to satisfy the external users' needs based on how they think. The KM approach includes different customers' solutions, such as product and services simulators and integration tools supporting several distribution channels.

The third example is the design of an enterprise portal as a KMS and knowledge delivery system. This design is meant to support the initiatives of content suites according to different audiences. The portal has the purpose of supporting transactions and applications. Some of the portal attributes are the capability to personalize, search capabilities, manage content, store and retrieve, organize and classify information and knowledge, integrate applications, facilitate collaboration as a way to transfer tacit knowledge, and enable single sign-on in order to navigate in only one environment with all the solutions

There are two main parts of the portal design with more priority: one is the identification of the knowledge to deliver, and the other is the means to deliver. These two points guide the development of a "portal of portals" in order to convert the portal as a KMS, including points such as those in textbox 10.2.

A particular point analyzed has been governance; this refers to the way a portal can be converted into a work tool for knowledge workers across the organization, supporting workflows. It needs support from the organization to develop the best way to create services for users where the users can take control of the next steps. The first exercise in governance definition was, using a metaphor, to compare a portal to a "commercial mall" where

---

TEXTBOX 10.2. POINTS TO INCLUDE IN THE PORTAL DESIGN: WHAT TO REVIEW AND PROCESSES

What to Review
- Channel integration
- Segmentation (speak to different audiences, providing them with targeted, focused content and information)
- Document management
- Operational efficiencies, flexibility, scalability
- Integration of systems
- Business intelligence (BI)
- Customer satisfaction, customer relationship management, customer loyalty, customer retention
- Business process management
- Empty portal factor and support to different audiences
- Access for stakeholders
- Focus on enhancing operational efficiency.
- Distribution channel strategy/ business development
- Intellectual/working capital solutions

Analysis of Processes
- Improve business alignment and partnerships.
- Clarify, improve, and communicate IT governance framework and practices.
- Enable the more effective capturing and sharing of intelligence across the corporation to provide better business solutions.
- Provide technology tools to enhance stakeholders' access to EDC's knowledge.
- Eliminate low-value activities in order to enhance productivity.
- Put more capability in the hands of our front-line service providers in order to grow the business.
- Optimize sales and service channels to increase customer satisfaction and acquisition, and decrease costs.
- Build IT capabilities to execute on EDC's partnership delivery model/strategy.
- Ramp up corporate capacity in the areas of strategic consulting; knowledge management; customer information management.

multiple users and multiple suppliers use the same kind of facilities in order to satisfy the customers. The metaphorical exercise was very useful in order to clarify how people, roles, and responsibilities can be associated with portals administration. This exercise was important in identifying the following roles and responsibilities: owner, steering committee, general manager, category and section managers, designers and developers, administrative support, promotion management, learning development, those responsible for usability and interface definitions, and metrics and analytics. All these roles preserve the principle of working together in order to deliver and maintain knowledge and transactions for different stakeholders.

EDC is in the process of reviewing a comprehensive portal strategy. The objectives and goals of implementing such a system must be clear to the entire corporation in order to achieve acceptance of the new strategy. In order to create corporatewide acceptance of the portal technology, the following points were considered important to address in the implementation:

- The portal's creation must be directly tied to business goals and objectives. This includes a review of the holistic view for knowledge access and collaboration.
- The comprehensive portal strategy should be a part of the enterprise IT strategy and should be led by the business.
- The strategy should quantify pragmatic and tangible results.
- The strategy should establish the governance as a cross-enterprise process.
- A single portal architecture that can allow multiple portals from different vendors must be in place across the entire enterprise.

A very important exercise was to use a prototype of the portal structure with all the components and features in order to review its value. It was based on the experiences and possible needs of the users. This exercise identified capabilities of software and at the same time the possibility of people from technology and people related to the business working on a common project, which in the organization was unique. The result was very valuable, and it opened the participants' minds about the capacity to connect business knowledge problems with solutions through a software infrastructure and as well as the ability of people from technology and business to work together in software evaluation.

The next step is to connect the portal with the KMS design and the capacity to provide business results in order to:

- increase employee productivity and cost avoidance
- reduce customer support costs
- increase revenues

- reduce IT costs
- gain a single point of access that results in a better use and high productivity
- automate processes and therefore reduce costs and improve accuracy

The overall goal of the enterprise portal is to deliver greater service to the "customer" at the same, or preferably, a lower cost.

The Challenge of Alignment of All Steps and Initiatives

Once the expected benefits of the initiatives have been identified, the next step is to align these initiatives with those EDC already has in place. The reason is that the initiatives are pieces of KM but with a possible development separation that can reduce the capacity of an integral view that shares principles of design and implementation.

This alignment can be seen as the organization of the "blocks of the blocks," required for helping to communicate to people the value of KM and the KMS. The KMS must be seen as something that is tangible in order for people to understand what KM is doing for them.

The challenge is to provide consistency to the "blocks of the blocks" and to the project blocks themselves, coordination of efforts, and consistency in the approaches to common goals. The main reason is that at the end people will see the value of the KM process as the KMS is built. This means that the enterprise architecture has a large part to play in the process of building a KMS and the way the different pieces have to be connected and supported.

The complexity is in sustaining, sharing, and communicating the common principles of KM among the different groups and initiatives already in place. Some of these projects are customer relationship management (CRM), content management, and business intelligence, developed independently and without a clear link to KM.

The alignment requires managing some attributes of technology, processes, and the people involved in the projects, such as:

- Preservation of the new integrative structure of the business for aligning knowledge production with consumption
- Definition of simple, customer-focused classifications for all knowledge, regions/countries/sectors, user goals, products, customer segments, entitlements, languages
- Movement from unstructured to structured/semistructured data
- Inventory of content and services
- Specification of portal features for different customer scenarios
- Implementation of structured cross-functional collaboration

Finally, the development of business intelligence activities and initiatives is very important, given the nature of this risk-based business. The use of the existing analytic tools and the data warehouse requires work to develop users, to share experiences, and to manage the same criteria and concepts. This is a challenge, given the variety of sources of external data and the way different departments use the data in reports and producing new knowledge.

CONCLUSION

The KM project provides value when it is part of the integration and application of knowledge in the development and support of EDC's business processes. The KM project requires a new governance view, risk strategy orientation, efficiency, and effectiveness in order to provide better and opportune solutions to grow the business. It has been introduced using the bottom-up approach, which starts incubating the KM processes with specific and clear applications instead of having a big KM organization and spending a lot of money in technology or resources.

The KM project has to represent for the business processes: capacity to support customers and to develop the business, simplification of the user's work, reduction of search steps, focus on the specific needs, capacity of knowledge consolidation, contribution to the organization of dispersed knowledge, development of a unique message and the structure to support it, and development of a capacity for working for a common objective in different areas. The phases of the KMS development are represented by the inclusion of new content and new tools for collaboration. The main point to take into consideration in the next stages is the access to internal and external users with collaboration tools to support tacit knowledge. There are other issues to solve in the next stages as well, such as document formats and structure, capacity for searching and managing virtual work across the organization, and capacity to share risk management experiences and decisions across the organization.

The application of the bottom-up strategy is very useful in order to show practical solutions and to create some credibility. However, it requires more time for implementation and the identification of sponsors for developing the KM applications. Moreover, coordination, alignment, and the indirect cost management require the support and involvement of executives in order to be more efficient and effective. Because there are many new initiatives across the organization, the bottom-up view reduces the capacity to coordinate the efforts and to apply common principles of design. In addition, it is crucial to preserve a solid theoretical framework and to educate decision makers and practitioners in order to provide capacity to connect all the pieces in a KM implementation.

Finally, there is an enormous field in which to do research in KM and its applications to several areas. A very important one, given the business, is risk management. For instance, it is important to work on identification of factors influencing the design of a KMS and the risk management information system, the capacity to provide KM support to the enterprise risk management processes, and the development of risk management knowledge workers in the organization.

REFERENCES

Alavi, M., and D. Leidner. 2001. "Review: Knowledge Management and Knowledge Management Systems: Conceptual Foundations and Research Issues." *MIS Quarterly* 25 (1): 107–36.
Nonaka, I., and H. Takeuchi. 1995. *The Knowledge-Creating Company: How Japanese Companies Create the Dynamics of Innovation.* New York: Oxford University Press.
Shaw, J. 2005. "Managing All Your Enterprise's Risks." *Risk Management* 52 (9): 22–30.
Warren, B. 2002. "What Is Missing from the RMIS Design? Why Enterprise Risk Management Is Not Working." *Risk Management,* October.

11

Viability of the Knowledge-Based Economic Paradigm

A Case Study of the Indian Economy

Ashish Dwivedi

Ashish Dwivedi

BACKGROUND ON THE HISTORY
OF THE KNOWLEDGE-BASED ECONOMY

There is widespread agreement that since the onset of the nineteenth century, human civilization has witnessed major changes in its economic systems. About sixty years ago, Hayek was among the earliest thinkers who brought to the forefront the importance of "knowledge" in an economic context when he stated that decisions are generally made upon dispersed bits of incomplete and frequently contradictory knowledge (Hayek 1945).

Today, we have shifted from an economy that was based upon traditional factors of production to an economy where the major factor of production is knowledge (Covin and Stivers 1997; Drucker 1993; Nonaka, Umemoto, and Senoo 1996). There is a growing body of literature focusing on the advent and impact of the new information age on the new economy of the millennium, which has been depicted as the Knowledge Economy (Vaitilingam 1999; Seybold 1995). These changes are summarized in table 11.1.

This chapter argues that this millennium shall witness a new economic world order—one that would be based upon knowledge that societies possess and not technology. This stand is supported by Stiglitz (1999) former senior vice president and chief economist of the World Bank and the Nobel Laureate for Economics in 2001. Stiglitz (1999, 38) had stated that

Table 11.1. Economic Evolutions. Adapted from Drucker (1993)

Economic Structures	*Industrial*	*Service*	*Knowledge*
Time frame	1850–1900	1920–1990	> 2000
Major factor of production	Land Labor	Capital Human Capital	Information
Dominant factor of production	Capital	Technology, Information	Knowledge
Major innovations	Steam Engine Railroad	Automobiles Microchip	Internet

one of the main reasons that the 1998 World Bank World Development Report was devoted to the theme of Knowledge for Development was due to the fact that the World Bank has recognized that they have to shift their emphasis so as to deal with the "intangibles of knowledge, institutions and culture."

Vaitilingam (1999) quotes the competitiveness white paper of the UK government to reiterate that in the new knowledge economy the most important factor influencing the creation of wealth would be the generation and exploitation of knowledge. Coates and Warwick (1999) quote the World Bank to mention that today the most important economies in the world are knowledge based. They also refer to the Organization for Economic Cooperation and Development (OECD) to say that the concept of knowledge-based economies engender new organizational orientations in employment, production, and human resource development.

A number of authors (Alavi and Leidner 2001; Grover and Davenport 2001; Zack 1999) have argued that the only way for an organization to thrive is to invest in its internal resources, particularly in the tacit knowledge of its employees and stakeholders and in existing organizational processes. This viewpoint has been labelled as the knowledge-based view (KBV) on strategic management.

The combined impact of the shift in our economic structures in conjunction with a shift in strategic management thought has resulted in two irrevocable changes in the modern day organizational landscape:

(1) Organizations are moving into an era wherein knowledge is the only resource/factor of production that can enable organizations to create and maintain sustainable competitive advantages

(2) Incorporation of KM as the new management mind-set by twenty-first-century organizations is essential for them, if they wish to make a successful transition to the knowledge economy of the future.

PROJECT DESCRIPTION: INDIAN ECONOMIC STRUCTURE

India, despite having 17.1 percent of the world's population, only possess about 1.8 percent of the world's gross domestic product (GDP) (see table 11.2). However, as per recent growth estimates, India's population is expected to become the largest in the world (EIU ViewsWire 2005a). This has resulted in tremendous pressure for creating employment opportunities. The challenge of providing employment to its ever-increasing population (see table 11.2) is being further exacerbated by the fact that in India, rates of rural underemployment and urban unemployment are high (EIU ViewsWire 2005a; 2005b).

Given the current difficulty that India faces in finding employment for its current working population, the entry of an extra 40–50 million people in the next five years as a consequence of a rise in India's working age population is likely to aggravate the challenge of providing employment to India's employable population (see table 11.3). It is clear that the challenge of providing employment is not going to be easy (EIU ViewsWire, 2005a).

Table 11.2.   India Income and Market Size (EIU ViewsWire 2005b)

Income and Market Size	2005	2010	2020	2030
Population (m)	1,095	1,170	1,315	1,442
GDP (US$ bn at market exchange rates)	763	1,238	3,328	9,341
GDP per capita (US$ at market exchange rates)	700	1,060	2,530	6,480
Exports of goods & services (US$ bn)	114	255	1,152	4,834
Imports of goods & services (US$ bn)	152	318	1,167	4,536
Share of world population (%)	17.1	17.3	17.7	18.1
Share of world GDP (% at market exchange rates)	1.8	2.3	3.4	5.2
Share of world exports (%)	0.9	1.4	3.0	5.9

Table 11.3.   India's Changes in Demographic Profile (EIU ViewsWire 2005a)

Demographic profile	1999	2004	2009
Population (m)			
Total	1,002.70	1,080.30	1,155.00
Male	518.6	557.4	594.5
Female	484.1	522.9	560.5
Age profile (% of total population)			
0–14	34	31.7	29.6
15–64	61.4	63.5	65.2
65+	4.6	4.8	5.2
Working-age population (m)	615.6	685.7	753.4
Urbanization (% of total)	27.4	29.2	30.3
Labor force (m)	440.4	486.6	533.6

India, in order to meet the challenge of creating more employment opportunities has to attract higher amounts of foreign direct investments, and
simultaneously ensure that it is able to obtain higher productivity from its
resources (both people and capital). Despite the fact that the government
led by the current prime minister, Manmohan Singh, has acknowledged
this issue (Kirkland 2005), no solution is in sight.

WHAT ACTUALLY HAPPENED—
EMERGENCE OF KM COMPANIES IN INDIA

The nations that will lead the world into the next century will be those that
can shift from being industrial economies based upon the production of
manufactured goods to those that possess the capacity to produce and utilize knowledge successfully (Porter 1990). Therefore the focal thrust of various economies has shifted first to information-intensive industries such as
financial services and logistics, and now toward innovation-driven industries, such as computer software and biotechnology, where competitive advantage lies primarily in the fostering and developing of unique ideas and
maximizing the potential of the human resources of organizations. The case
of the Indian software industry fully illustrates this example.

The Indian software industry, in less than a decade, has emerged as a key
player in the global information technology (IT) industry and in the software industry in particular (Asundi 2001; Biswas 2001; Landi 2003; Nirjar
and Tylecote 2005). In 1993–1994, India's revenues from software exports
were about US$558 million, which by 2001 had shot up to about $8.5 billion and to $17.5 billion by 2004–2005 (Asundi 2001; National Associa-
tion of Software and Services Companies 2002, 2003; Nirjar and Tylecote
2005). The software industry in India has grown at an astonishing rate of
over 50 percent annually from 1994 to 1999 (Biswas 2001; Contractor,
Hsu, and Kundu 2005; Nirjar and Tylecote 2005) and from 1999 to 2002 at
over 26 percent annually (Nirjar and Tylecote 2005) with expectations that
its revenues will hit the $50 billion mark by 2008 (National Association of
Software and Services Companies 2002, 2003; Nirjar and Tylecote 2005).

The success of India's IT sector has promoted India's policy makers to attempt to transform the Indian economy to a knowledge-based economy.
This chapter therefore examines the feasibility of the knowledge-based economic model as an appropriate economic model for developing countries
like India that have a huge population.

According to Chandler (2005) as recently as twenty years ago both India
and China were on "roughly equal footing. Both were large, predominantly
agrarian countries with GDPs of less than $1 trillion and per capita incomes
of about $300. Today China's economy is more than twice as large as In-

dia's and is posting average annual growth rates of 9 percent to 10 percent, compared with India's 6 percent to 7 percent. Per capita income in China is now more than double what it is in India. . . . China takes in 12 times as much in annual foreign direct investment as India ($60 billion vs. $5 billion), and it exports almost six times as much each year ($600 billion vs. $105 billion)."

A large part of China's success can be attributed to the improvements made in the manufacturing sector and the physical infrastructure to support the manufacturing sector. India, on the other hand has not been able to improve its manufacturing sector. By and large, India's manufacturing sector suffers from red tape, bureaucratic hurdles, restrictive labor laws, expensive power supplies, and poor infrastructure (EIU ViewsWire 2005b). India's current government—the UPA government—continues to focus on the agricultural sector and in manufacturing prefers the manufacturing sector to utilize the wider, less well-educated workforce (EIU ViewsWire 2005b), which incidentally is the exact opposite of what the private sector desires in India.

An analysis of recent Indian manufacturing sector success stories like Bajaj Automotive and Bharat Forge indicate that their success could be traced to a shift in their economic model. They have shifted from an economic model that emphasized maximizing production and revenues using large production workforces who were semiskilled and worked on low wages to an economic model where there is a vastly reduced workforce that is highly skilled and highly paid, and uses the latest technology (Chandler 2005). The resultant change in productivity is tremendous, as illustrated by the following two examples.

In the early 1990s, Bajaj Automotive built 1 million vehicles with 24,000 semiskilled, low-wage workers. Now, Bajaj Automotive currently builds 2.4 million vehicles with a vastly reduced workforce of 10,500 that is highly skilled and highly paid. In fact, it has been noted that Bajaj Automotive would be in a position to run an even leaner operation if the government would give it permission to do so (Chandler 2005).

Another example that illustrates the impact between the two economic models is the case of Bharat Forge, currently India's most successful auto-parts supplier. Bharat has the world's largest single-site forging facility. In 1996, the CEO of Bharat Forge noted that using his low-cost, semiskilled workforce, the company was only able to raise productivity by 20 percent (under optimum conditions).

Bharat Forge then decided to shift to an economic model that used an elite cadre of highly skilled workers and current technology. (Over 600 of his original 1,800 workers were given financial incentives to retire and then replaced by vastly superior qualified workers who are paid substantially more.) The result: instead of looking at productivity gains of about

20 percent, Bharat Forge was able to obtain productivity gains of 400 percent (Chandler 2005).

Another case that highlights the importance of using an economic model that emphasizes vastly superior qualified workers is the case of the Indian IT industry. The annual software exports from the Indian IT industry have risen from almost nonexistent levels to about $15 billion in about a decade and is predicted to reach $87 billion by 2008 (Chandler 2005).

These cases clearly illustrate that to survive in the global market place, Indian companies have to shift their economic model to one that emphasizes smaller, highly skilled workforces who use the latest technology and consequently are paid higher wages—a point also reiterated by the worldwide shift in academic thought on strategic management.

Given the current trend in both management thought and success stories of Indian companies using knowledge as the key source of competitive advantage, it can be argued that in the future, only those Indian companies that employ highly skilled workforces will survive and, indeed, thrive in the global market place. However, it will also be a significant challenge for the captains of India's economic, industrial, and political bastions to be able to make the change to this new model.

The focus for employers like the Indian IT sector, the multinationals, and Indian organizations such as Bharat Forge and Bajaj Automotive will be on employing workers who are highly skilled. However, while the coming age of knowledge-based industries will be very beneficial for a certain segments of the Indian economy, it might not be an appropriate economic model for the entire Indian economy. The main reason for this lies in the fact that the application of the knowledge-based-economy model in India, as evidenced by its application in India's IT and manufacturing sectors, would only provide employment for a small, privileged section of India's population. An indicator of this can be seen in the fact that currently there are only about 1 million skilled-job opportunities in India's knowledge industries (Chandler 2005) while the total working-age population in India is about 440 million (EIU ViewsWire 2005a).

Application of the knowledge-based economic model in its current form would also mean that a large section of the Indian working-age population would likely be employed in low-wage jobs or be unemployed, which in turn would further accentuate the urban-rural, skilled-unskilled workers divide, resulting in widening the rich-poor divide for the middle class in India.

Failure to come up with a knowledge-based economic model that is customized to India's population, culture, and ethos could be detrimental to India, and would result in a scenario wherein by 2030 India's poverty will continue to exist, despite having an estimated average per capita GDP (US$ at market exchange rates) of $6,500, up from $700 in 2005 (EIU ViewsWire 2005b).

Sadly, the captains of India's economic bastions have not recognized this fact. Nandan M. Nilekani, CEO of Infosys, observes that in the knowledge economy, markets will trade in what has long been untradable "workers' education and skills," and that economic growth will be driven by the capacity of economies to create knowledge and innovate (Nilekani 2006). He goes on to remark that "India has poor infrastructure, low literacy levels for many people, and labour inflexibilities," and hence high-volume manufacturing (akin to China) has not taken off yet in a big way (Nilekani 2006). This clearly implies that the future will call for skilled workers, and this would require high literacy levels among the population (typically not present in developing countries like India). At the same time, no solution is offered to the key challenge: how to customize the knowledge-based economic model to India's employable population of over 400 million.

SUCCESSES AND FAILURES

Another dilemma facing Indian conglomerates in the quest to shift to a knowledge-based economic model relates to creating a culture that supports knowledge sharing. Except for the Indian IT sector, which was forced to develop a knowledge-sharing culture in order to survive, none of the other Indian industrial sectors have adopted mechanisms that promote/develop a knowledge-sharing culture as a key organizational theme. In the 1990s, a number of Indian outsourcing firms adopted the "Capability Maturity Model" (CMM), which necessities open sharing and comparing processes. Adoption of CMM and creation of a knowledge-sharing culture enabled Indian companies to "establish credibility, reduced risks for overseas buyers and made future sales easier" (Boisot 2006).

Though there is widespread agreement among academics that sharing knowledge is essential, and the Indian IT companies have gained by it, most Indian companies do not know their knowledge assets and, more significantly, have not attempted to either identify or articulate them. For example, India is one of the world's leading diamond centers, and consequently the Indian diamond industry receives raw diamond stones from South Africa and Russia, which have to be cut and polished. The entire diamond industry in India is dominated by one caste (i.e., a particular social group): the Jain community, who hail from Surat, a small town in the state of Gujarat. Furthermore, they use angadias (people from a specific caste) as their couriers, not professional companies like DHL. Like the diamond merchants (i.e., the Jain community), the trade secrets of the angadias are not known. However, there is a widely held perception that any item given to an angadia will always be safely delivered. Most important, one has to belong to their community to be allowed to work as either an angadia or as a diamond merchant. The implication is clear: caste cannot be ignored in India (Boisot 2006).

Ravi Trivedy, director of e-Business and IT Strategy at Pricewaterhouse Coopers (PwC), has noted that few Indian companies have adopted a knowledge culture, and Ajoy Kurup, human resources manager at Kale Consultants, adds that "in theory, most Indian companies have a clear understanding of the difference between information and knowledge. But in practice the lines are blurred." (Anonymous 2001).

The late Peter Drucker, the noted management thinker, also supported the notion being put forward by Indian CEOs such as Nandan M. Nilekani and academic thought (resource-based view and knowledge-based view) when he stated that knowledge workers are exceedingly specialized, and that their knowledge has to be integrated into a team of knowledge workers (Anonymous 2005). This is going to be difficult for any developing country like India due to its literacy level and the population and industrial demographics. According to Muruganandan (2004), the research agency Evalueserve has predicted that by 2010 the global high-end business process outsourcing (BPO) market will be worth $50 billion, and it projects that India's market share is likely to be around $30 billion (i.e., 60 percent market share). However, the lack of a skilled manpower base is already crippling India's BPO market. According to the accounting firm KPMG, more than a million people would be required by 2008 to meet the BPO demand, but supply will fall short by more than 250,000 (Muruganandan 2004).

The challenge facing developing countries like India is how to convert their huge population base into a pool of knowledge workers, and given the fact that future knowledge industries will require a smaller number of highly skilled knowledge workers, the knowledge-based economy could be the Achilles heel for the developing countries.

EPILOGUE

The chapter has argued that the rise of the knowledge-based economic paradigm can be traced to the coming of age of two key forces: (a) shift in the economic structures and (b) evolution in strategic management thought. The combined impact of these two drivers has further brought about two irrevocable changes in the modern-day organizational landscape: (1) organizations are moving into an era where knowledge is the only resource/factor of production that can enable them to create and maintain sustainable competitive advantages and (2) that incorporation of KM as the new management mind-set by the twenty-first-century organization is essential for them to make a successful transition to the knowledge economy of the future.

This chapter has reviewed the impact of knowledge as a factor of production on developing countries. The Indian economy is adopted as a case study to illustrate the impact of creating a knowledge-based economy. The findings indicate that by 2030, despite a marked increase in Indian per capita GDP (which is likely to be led by India' knowledge industries such as its software industry), there is the possibility that India will continue to suffer from widespread poverty. Consequently, this chapter argues that the knowledge-based economic model may not be an appropriate economic model for developing countries like India that have a huge population. There is a need to explore innovative mechanisms of combining knowledge-based employment opportunities with industries that can employ India's ever-increasing population in a productive manner.

The chapter concludes by arguing that the captains of India's economic, industrial, and political bastions need to recognize this challenge. Solutions to this problem will require an honest, sustained, and committed dialogue between the captains of India's economic, industrial, and political bastions.

REFERENCES

Alavi, M., and D. Leidner. 2001. "Knowledge Management and Knowledge Management Systems: Conceptual Foundations and Research Issues." *MIS Quarterly* 25 (1): 107–36.

Anonymous. 2001. "India: Treasure Hunt." *Businessline*, 1.

Anonymous. 2005. "Thought Leadership: Peter Drucker—a Lifetime of Wisdom." *New Zealand Management*, 42.

Asundi, J. 2001. *Issues in Software Development: Outsourcing, Design and Organisation.* Unpublished PhD dissertation, Carnegie Mellon University.

Biswas, R. R. 2001. *Hyderabad: Technopolis in the Making? A Study of the Software Industry in Hyderabad, Anhdra Pradesh, India and the Andhra Pradesh Information Technology Policy.* Unpublished MA thesis, University of Massachusetts–Lowell.

Boisot, M. 2006. "How Much Knowledge Should a Business Give Away?" *European Business Forum* 24:7–8.

Chandler, C. 2005. "India's Bumpy Ride." *Fortune* 152 (9): 135–47.

Coates, D., and K. Warwick. 1999. "The Knowledge-Driven Economy: Analysis and Background." Presented at The Economics of the Knowledge Driven Economy, London, 11–21.

Contractor, F. J., C. C. Hsu, and S. K. Kundu. 2005. "Explaining Export Performance: A Comparative Study of International New Ventures in Indian and Taiwanese Software Industry." *Management International Review* 45(3): 83–110.

Covin, T. J., and B. P. Stivers. 1997. "Knowledge Management in Focus in UK and Canadian Firms." *Creativity and Innovation Management* 6 (3): 140–50.

Drucker, P. F. 1993. "The Rise of the Knowledge Society." *Wilson Quarterly* 17 (2): 52–70.

EIU ViewsWire. 2005a. "India Economy: India's Population Expected to Become Largest in the World." September 29.

EIU ViewsWire. 2005b. "India Economy: Ten-Year Growth Outlook." August 26.

Grover, V., and T. H. Davenport. 2001. "General Perspectives on Knowledge Management: Fostering a Research Agenda." *Journal of Management Information Systems* 18 (1): 5–21.

Hayek, F. A. 1945. "The Use of Knowledge in Society." *American Economic Review* 35 (4): 519–30.

Kirkland, R. 2005. "Riding the Elephant." *Fortune* 152 (9): 148.

Landi, C. M. 2003. *Constructing Comparative Advantage: How India Is Moving Up the Global Software Value Chain.* Unpublished PhD dissertation, The American University.

Muruganandan, G. 2004 "How Boom Can Go Bust." *Businessline* (December 20), 1.

National Association of Software and Services Companies. 2002. *The IT Industry in India: Strategic Review.* Delhi: National Association of Software and Services Companies.

National Association of Software and Services Companies. 2003. *The IT Industry in India: Strategic Review.* Delhi: National Association of Software and Services Companies.

Nilekani, N. M. 2006. "In Asia." *Business Week* 4002:36.

Nirjar, A., and A. Tylecote. 2005. "Breaking Out of Lock-In: Insights from Case Studies into Ways Up the Value Ladder for Indian Software SMEs." *Information Resources Management Journal* 18 (4): 40–61.

Nonaka, I., K. Umemoto, and D. Senoo. 1996. "From Information Processing to Knowledge Creation: A Paradigm Shift in Business Management." *Technology in Society* 18 (2): 203–18.

Porter, M. E. 1990. *The Competitive Advantage of Nations.* New York: Free Press.

Seybold, P. B. 1995. "Preparing for the Knowledge Economy." *Chief Executive* 100:18.

Stiglitz, J. E. 1999. "Knowledge in the Modern Economy." Presented at The Economics of the Knowledge Driven Economy. Centre for Economic Policy Research, London, 37–55.

Vaitilingam, R. 1999 "Overview: The Economics of the Knowledge-Driven Economy." Presented at The Economics of the Knowledge Driven Economy. Centre for Economic Policy Research, London, 5–10.

Zack, M. H. 1999. "Managing Codified Knowledge." *Sloan Management Review* 40 (4): 45–58.

12

The Value of Knowledge Management in a Federal Agency

Laura Moore and Denise Lee

In the U.S. federal government environment, providing value does not necessarily mean the same thing as it does in the private sector. Therefore, when reflecting on "making cents out of knowledge management" it does not necessarily mean only money. That is not to say that saving money in the government is not important; nor does it imply that we are not accountable, just that it is couched in "using tax payer dollars judiciously." For instance, annual reporting of performance measures is required as part of the Office of Management and Budget's (OMB) oversight of government spending. There is much less of a focus on profit and more on providing the best value to our federal customer agencies and ultimately to the taxpayer. Again, "competitive intelligence" in the federal space does not have the same connotations either, but can be framed as less focus on the competitive, more focus on the intelligence aspects necessary to deliver on our mission.

BACKGROUND

The General Services Administration (GSA) Public Buildings Service (PBS) is the largest public real estate organization in the nation and a provider of workspace and workplace solutions to more than 100 federal government departments and agencies. PBS has developed and implemented strategic programs that will transform it into a more customer-focused provider of government workplaces. In 2004 PBS initiated a knowledge management program to address the creation, capture, and retention of knowledge capital. The PBS Office of Applied Science's Knowledge Management (KM) Division is responsible for the Enterprise Knowledge Management Program. The PBS KM Division is tasked with developing the collaborative knowledge resources that support the PBS workforce.

Conducting a Knowledge Management Survey

A knowledge management survey was conducted in 2005 through the PBS Office of Applied Science Knowledge Management Division. A sample of 629 employees throughout PBS was surveyed through a quantitative web-based survey containing sixty-six questions. The questions in the survey explored PBS perceptions regarding the following:

- Need for knowledge management
- Levels of knowledge management effectiveness
- Current knowledge management initiatives
- Factors contributing to knowledge management in the organization

Following the survey, respondents were invited to participate in focus groups. Ninety-three PBS employees were interviewed to further collect observations and recommendations regarding knowledge management practices at PBS.

The results of the survey indicated that PBS was an organization positioned to appreciate and leverage the value of knowledge management. According to survey results, PBS relied on experience and know-how (i.e., tacit knowledge) more than on explicit, codified knowledge. Therefore, the survey indicated that many strong social networks already existed within PBS. For the most part, these tend to be functionally oriented. For example, active social networks existed with a focus on real estate, project management, regional procurement, real property asset management (RPAM), contracts, customer service, and budget. The Knowledge Management Division, building on the results from the survey, determined that their focus should be:

- Collaboration: responsible for business/cultural considerations, functional requirements, and change-management processes
- Content: provides the methods and structure for information/resource capture, organization, and presentation
- Media: provides the technology and architectural enablers for collaborative environments

There were targeted elements of the current environment to be improved in order to maximize the success of the knowledge management initiatives and to further leverage the benefits of the cultural and structural strengths of PBS. Additionally, the strengths of the PBS culture and processes could be leveraged to accelerate the rate of knowledge exchange and innovation with the application specific technologies in specific manners.

PBS KM Board of Governors

Realizing that KM shouldn't operate in a vacuum and there was a need for strong senior management guidance and support, four well-respected, senior PBS executives and the deputy PBS commissioner, in an advisory capacity, formed the first PBS KM Board of Governors. The importance of forming this board rested on the needed to have access to a group of senior executives from whom to seek guidance and approval on KM initiatives as the project moved forward.

STRATEGY

Knowledge management is a set of systematic approaches that help information and knowledge to flow to the right people at the right time and in the right format at the right cost, allowing employees to act more efficiently and effectively to create value. The Knowledge Management Division exists so that PBS will be able to improve the identification of important knowledge, to create a space and process for PBS employees to share what they know. A well-respected member of the KM Governance Board, Mr. Glenn S. Hunter, assistant commissioner of the Office of Applied Science, clarifies, "When the KM Division was formed in my office I recognized the value it could bring to PBS through leveraging our collective knowledge."

The PBS Knowledge Management strategy was to create a program that is defined and shaped by the PBS strategy to be *the preferred provider of world-class workplace solutions for the federal customer agencies*. The PBS knowledge management program establishes a centralized common body of intellectual capital to drive consistent and high-quality decision making and problem solving. Specifically within PBS, the knowledge management strategy is targeted at three basic value statements.

1. A common knowledge repository provides increased consistency, quality, and collaboration. Knowledge management will establish and maintain a centralized knowledge repository, which PBS is currently lacking. By establishing this resource, PBS will achieve heightened awareness, increased consistency, and greater collaboration.
2. The integration of knowledge management and process management (process-centric KM) increases consistency, quality, and timeliness.

This integration will create a system in which relevant and just-in-time knowledge is made available to process executors, which results in increased rate of response, constancy in responses, and thus quality of responses.

3. Knowledge management services facilitate and nurture collaboration across PBS to increase quality and consistency. These services and infrastructure will support teams and communities of practice (CoPs) within and across PBS, thus allowing for "good ideas" and/or best practices to be easily shared and absorbed across the organization.

The purpose of this strategy was to create a cyclical system in which intelligent knowledge workers would seek and share knowledge. They would then utilize it in the performance of their respective processes, which would result in the accumulation of additional know-how and knowledge. The project leaders were seeking to create a learning organization that continually grows smarter and more responsive. This led to the realization that ultimately it should be appreciated within PBS that knowledge management should not be positioned as an initiative or project, per se, but rather as a series of ongoing services and functions. Thus knowledge management strategy is modular in nature.

IMPLEMENTATION

The three projects discussed below tie directly to the key strategic elements of:

1. Strategic alignment to PBS business goals
2. Access to enterprise knowledge assets
3. Knowledge delivered via targeted task and processes
4. Empowering collaboration

Initial PBS KM efforts focused on empowering collaboration, as a collaborative culture and technological tools to support it were already in place.

Project 1: After Action Reviews and Retrospects—Hurricane Katrina

After Action Reviews (AAR) and Retrospects are examples of *action learning*: learning that results from experience. This experience could be, for example, discussions among participants of a project, operation, or other professional event. The participants meet after the event to learn from their experience and from this discussion may draw conclusions: For example, how can we strengthen practices that were successful? How can we improve practices that fell short?

In 2005, in the aftermath of Hurricane Katrina, there was an opportunity to employ this KM practice and principle—AAR—in a very tactical manner. Several of PBS's customer agencies had a presence in the Gulf Coast area, and because of the complete devastation wrought by Hurricane Katrina, their government workspaces were uninhabitable. It was the knowledge management team's mission to get these agencies up and operational, even in temporary space, as quickly as possible. Therefore in the wake of this disaster, the idea was for the team leaders to travel to the Gulf Coast while rebuilding was underway and the experience was still fresh. The project was to assist PBS regional staff in the development of a Disaster Recovery Standard Operating Procedures Manual (SOP) to be used by PBS regions that routinely have to deal with hurricanes or any natural disaster response.

The team travelled to Gulf Port, Mississippi, to directly capture the lessons learned and best practices that the regional staff used in the response to Katrina. Kyle S. Edwards, one of the team leaders, explains, "We used the After Action Review and Retrospect methodologies to gather the knowledge from this event. We then took these interviews, did follow-up focus groups, and developed a robust manual. The value of this project was that it was recognized as a significant tool on front lines of PBS disaster response and that its use would help to minimize customer impact due to loss of access to their workplace."

Project 2: Collaborative Spaces

One important knowledge management collaborative initiative that is currently underway is the support for virtual teams and communities of practice in collaborative spaces on the PBS portal. As PBS moves forward with its transformation to become more customer-centric, establishing enterprise collaborative spaces is one way to achieve this goal. In order to fully realize the power of collaboration people need to be set in place with a standard methodology, a standard lexicon, and a standard toolkit. In support of this effort PBS's knowledge management team brought on board a collaboration specialist, Loeala Hammons, to bring together a collaborative environment at PBS.

PBS employees access the collaborative environment through the PBS Enterprise Portal. In 2006, Team Central and Community Central were launched. Kyle Edwards, collaboration team leader, comments, "These were entry points into an online environment that would support the strategic element of moving PBS toward a learning organization."

These entry points offered PBS employees access to functions such as:

- Collaborative spaces
- Discussions forums

- Instant messaging
- Document management
- Centralized content management

Hammons comments, "These entry points provide a centralized place where PBS employees can connect with other like-minded individuals interested in practices (such as realty, property management, etc.) and work processes to share, exchange, and reuse knowledge that is vital to meeting the mission of the PBS organization."

These spaces are for collaborating around topics such as:

- Debating the trade-offs of different approaches to capturing and using best practices
- Identification of, and alignment and coordination with, various regional KM efforts
- Strategies for maximizing the effectiveness of collaboration technologies

The KM team also began conducting a review and collection of their own lessons learned as they deployed these collaborative environments. They were constantly listening to their internal PBS customers, which supported the strategy of becoming a learning organization by continuously circulating reflection through their work. The value of these collaborative environments is the sharing of knowledge between employees that enables the dissemination of lessons learned and best practices that will ultimately lead to an improvement in service to the customer. An important aspect of that is listening to the customer. At the PBS Knowledge Division there is a focus on customer service. Sandy Wells, director of Human Capital Organizational Effectiveness, shares, "I felt a real connection to this project from its inception. My team and I were invited to internal KM meetings to contribute to both design and development phases. This collaboration ensured a broad range of thinking and ideas—an important ingredient to create a more fully developed product. Not only is the product better, but inclusion in the early phases helps ensure the support that is needed for implementation."

Project 3: PBS Knowledge Exchange (PKE)

The PBS Knowledge Exchange (PKE) will be the tactical implementation of the key strategic elements of accessing knowledge and delivering that knowledge through a process-centric methodology. This project has been in development during 2007 and is targeted to rollout in 2008. The development phase of a project on this scale includes strategic planning, taxonomy and content management elements, and a robust implementation plan. An important component is also maintaining a strong relationship with the

PBS CIO. Edward Meyman, PBS Portal Project manager, explains, "The PKE will be an integrated environment of processes and technology for capturing, collecting, and accessing PBS working knowledge such as good practices, lessons learned, and other work-related content." The collaboration with the CIO is an essential component to any successful knowledge management endeavor especially one on the scale of the PKE.

Edwards points out, "The PKE will hold vetted and unvetted content of many knowledge types; including, lessons learned, job aids, case studies, stories, best practices, customer information, and meeting minutes/conference notes. When fully developed, the PKE will permit users to rank the value of individual knowledge artifacts, direct subject matter experts to vet content, and allow users to post conversations attached to individual pieces of content."

Knowledge delivery is a major component of the PKE. The PKE will allow for two major elements of the KM strategy: access to knowledge and process-centric knowledge delivery. Access to knowledge is the *pull* aspect of knowledge delivery, and process-centric knowledge delivery is the *push* aspect, that is, getting the right information to the right person at the right time in a manner that is targeted to specific tasks and processes. An example of some of the types of knowledge in the PKE are as follows:

- Best/good practices
- Standard operating procedures
- Lessons learned
- Stories
- Case studies
- Sample/example
- Process/procedure
- Research

This architecture will provide value to PBS by:

- Providing a clearinghouse for operational groups to share and build useful knowledge
- Facilitating the sharing of knowledge across organizational, geographic, and functional boundaries
- Providing a means to get the right knowledge to the right person, at the right time
- Reducing content duplication

As PBS moves forward in its goal of becoming a trusted partner with its customers and a provider of world-class workplaces, the KM Division is in a unique position to greatly assist PBS in overcoming barriers to knowledge exchange.

IMPACT

Measuring the performance or direct value of knowledge management programs remains a challenge. Gathering and reporting meaningful measures is as much an art as it is a science, and one needs to put a stake in the ground. Organizations cannot wait for the thought leaders in this discipline to come up with the perfect way to measure. They have to develop a set of measures that make sense for their own operations. It is better to start off with a not-so-exact set of KM measures and to constantly refine than it is to wait until a perfect solution emerges. The measures in PBS's case align with their KM strategic elements of enabling and facilitating collaboration and knowledge delivery in a rough, but nevertheless real and meaningful manner.

In the federal government, performance measures have specific rules and requirements that govern them. For instance, some government programs have a mandate to report their performance measures to an oversight authority such as the Office of Management and Budget. In the case of the PBS KM program, the reporting is strictly internal to PBS and the parent organization GSA. To that end, the PBS Office of Applied Science manages via a dashboard methodology for all of the programs that fall under their jurisdiction. Hunter states, "I believe that the use of these dashboards is a valuable and practical tool for us to make decisions regarding our programs."

The PBS KM Division developed a dashboard in accordance with the requirement of the Office of Applied Science. For all the programs under the Office of Applied Science, definitions, measures, targets, and measurement intervals were developed. For the KM program, measures were developed to address the performance and impact of the collaboration environment and the use of the PBS Knowledge Exchange, and they contain the following components:

1. Number of virtual teams and CoPs
2. Customer satisfaction scores with teams and CoPs
3. PBS total awareness of teams and CoPs
4. Number of artifacts in the PBS Knowledge Exchange

The first three metrics are assessed via a survey of members of the teams and CoPs at approximately one-quarter of the user base. The last metric is assessed automatically when artifacts are accessed via the PBS Knowledge Exchange.

Some specific measures for 2006 are:

- 50 collaborative spaces brought online
- 39 of the collaborative spaces are headed from headquarters with a national scope
- 300 new members

- 11 regions supported
- 3 major business functions served
- 5 distinct national programs

SUCCESSES AND FAILURES

The PBS Knowledge Management Division always looks for creative ways to share its successes. One such innovative method is the use of storytelling. Text box 12.1 contains an example of the kind of success story the KM Division used at every opportunity to infuse story into its work.

TEXTBOX 12.1. SITUATION AND RELATED PBS KM PROGRAM RESOURCES

Dave is a program analyst. He has just been designated as a team lead on a project in which he will need the expertise of PBS employees across the country. Dave quickly pulls out his rolodex and leaves voicemail messages to the six other regional contacts that are a part of his project. After a week, he has heard back from two contacts, but they were voicemails because he had missed their calls. Dave sends out a blanket e-mail and awaits responses from his contacts. Dave quickly becomes frustrated with this whole process and thinks to himself, "There has got to be a better way."

Dave talks to Sheryl, his program counterpart in HQ, about his situation because he knows she had a similar role a couple of months ago.

Sheryl explained to Dave that she had formed a Virtual Team. After an hour of training provided by the PBS KM Division, Sheryl and the rest of her nationwide team were able to participate in discussion forums and online chats, post meetings on the calendar, and post and retrieve documents through libraries.

Sheryl also mentioned to Dave that her Virtual Team used the After Action Review (AAR) process to determine lessons learned at various stages of the project, and preliminary best practices, and to document their lessons learned. She learned how to do an AAR from a course PBS KM offered through the GSA On-Line University.

Sheryl showed Dave their lessons learned so that Dave could see what worked for her group, what did not work for her group, and how he could apply those practices and lessons to his new group. Sheryl also mentioned to Dave that she knew there were a couple of communities of practice already working, and since there were so many PBS employees who had a long-term need to share information and collaborate beyond just the scope of their respective teams, she was thinking about contacting the PBS KM Division to discuss developing a CoP for their work area.

Dave then went on to contact the KM Division and set up his own Virtual Team.

In any program there is always the opportunity to gather lessons learned. Rob Graf, PBS assistant regional administrator for Washington State and member of the KM Governance Board counsels, "Your connection with business processes is critical at the program level, and to the extent you can identify a technology or process that can have an immediate positive impact, focus on that. But if programmatic collaboration is to succeed, you will continue to need to find a way to get senior management commitment and involvement." Therefore, there needs to be awareness that trying to move a knowledge management program forward is always a risky endeavor. Unfortunately, there continues to be a lack of understanding of the value and benefit KM can bring to an enterprise. As this program's dear friend and colleague, Melissie Rumizen, KM expert, has stated many times, KM is where IT was fifteen or twenty years ago, and one no longer has to explain to people what IT is or its value. KM will be there one day too.

13

The NASA PBMA Knowledge Management Program

J. Steven Newman and Stephen M. Wander

BACKGROUND, HISTORY, AND CASE DESCRIPTION

The National Aeronautics and Space Administration (NASA) Office of Safety and Mission Assurance (OSMA) began development and deployment of a pioneering knowledge management (KM) system (KMS) that was designed to support the NASA/OSMA core function of enabling safety and mission success for all NASA programs, projects, facilities, and operations. PBMA stands for "Process-Based Mission Assurance," a process-oriented approach to safety and mission assurance (SMA) developed during the mid-1990s from benchmarking government and aerospace industry best practices and implementation of "advanced-quality" programs. While originally developed with an SMA focus, this pathfinder effort has grown into an agencywide KM program with a broad portfolio of services, products, and activities designed to stimulate and enable collaboration, communication, organizational learning, and innovation. Figure 13.1 is a snapshot of the dynamic and evolving "Home Page."

IMPLEMENTATION APPROACH

The PBMA-KMS (http://pbma.nasa.gov) was tactically implemented combining a practical application of KM theory, a systems engineering management

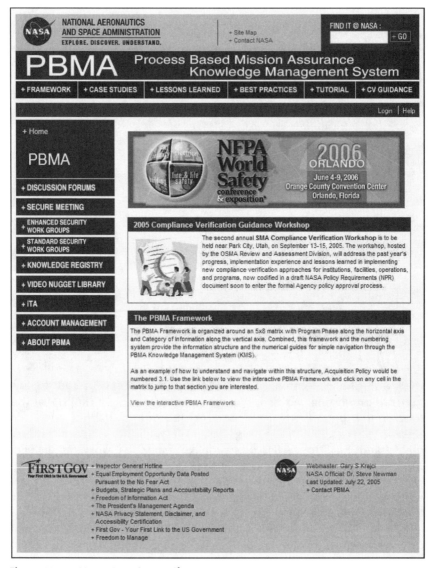

Figure 13.1.   Home Page Screen Shot

approach, and a continual-improvement/risk-management philosophy. The theoretical basis, a four-pillar KM framework (leadership, organization, technology, and learning) was provided by the George Washington University Knowledge Management Program under the direction of Professor Michael Stankosky. This model provided a starting point and underpinning for the initial concept development and internal marketing effort. The PBMA-KMS implementation was undertaken by a team of systems engineers within a systems engineering organization and was well served by observing systems engineering principles and practices. As an initial step, the PBMA-KMS management team actively engaged all relevant stakeholders, with the principal stakeholders being the SMA and program/project communities. Secondary stakeholders include agency IT security, agency security, ITAR/export control managers, human resource managers, the chief engineer/systems engineering, and training organizations. The focus of this approach was to individually address stakeholder requirements, needs, and objectives; explore potential synergies with ongoing activities; and identify bounding or constraining issues. For example, the management team forged a close partnership with the chief information officer (CIO), agency IT security, export control, and external-affairs organizations to discover what it takes to meet their requirements. In other words, the management team set out to build and operate PBMA-KMS on the basis of "compliance by design."

Strategic Alignment / Sponsorship

The PBMA-KMS strategic alignment was always (and continues to be) an important factor in the success. The overarching vision was "sold" to a very powerful sponsor/advocate, Bryan O'Connor, chief safety and mission assurance officer (CSMAO), who is a direct report to the NASA administrator. The CSMAO is also the associate administrator for the OSMA, an important, independently funded, functional support organization with responsibilities that extend across all NASA centers, programs, and facilities. It is important to note that the PBMA-KMS originated within this functional support organization and was neither directed nor mandated (or for that matter even initially supported) by the CIO/IT organizational infrastructure.

PBMA-KMS PROGRAM ELEMENTS

The program elements discussed below include (1) the knowledge architecture and user interfaces; (2) content development and management; (3) collaboration functionality; (4) IT infrastructure; (5) IT security; and (6) human interaction, group dynamics, and organizational learning.

Knowledge Architecture

The PBMA-KMS knowledge architecture (KA), shown in figure 13.2, was structured around the NASA program/project management and systems-engineering development life cycle, which consists of the eight elements of program management, concept development, acquisition, hardware design, software design, manufacturing, preoperations integration and test, and operations/disposal. The KA also incorporates the management dimensions of policies, plans, processes, controls, and verification, which closely corresponds to Deming's classic model of "plan, do, check, act." This KA vision is designed to help program/project management teams perform core functions in a more effective manner; accordingly, the KA reflects program/project core work flow and work processes. The resulting 8×5 matrix is intended to serve as a point of reference not only for planning and implementing new programs but also for conducting independent evaluations of existing programs.

It is also important to note that different business units and work functions will require their own unique KAs. To this end, the PBMA-KMS management team is currently developing multiple KA frameworks to provide greater utility to the user community. These include architectures based on engineering disciplines, program/project milestone gates, science mission functions, and system/subsystem/elements (see figure 13.3). The important thing to recognize is that a rich and robust set of knowledge artifacts (documents, written and verbal text, videos, and images) can reside on knowledge-based servers and be brought forward and served in a variety of different, user-intuitive formats.

Content, Content, Content

The knowledge-base for PBMA-KMS has been populated with core agency SMA policies and requirements; systems engineering, risk management, and knowledge management concepts; best practices; lessons learned; case studies; hundreds of links; and video nuggets (i.e., tacit knowledge capture via video interviews with experts). Once in place, core "killer content" can serve well in the quasi-stable world of engineering principles and practices. At the same time, we realized that the fast-paced web environment is one that demands constant refresh and renewal to keep users engaged. Accordingly, our content management strategy has evolved to incorporate expanding dynamic content with videos, updates, case studies, and evolutionary organizational learning content on the home page, supported, as always, by the "killer content" within the knowledge base.

Collaboration and Communication

The PBMA-KMS introduced NASA to secure, web-based communities of practice (CoPs) to enable unprecedented communication and collaboration opportunities to foster safety and mission success, and it has taken a lead in identifying needs within NASA for these secured collaborative

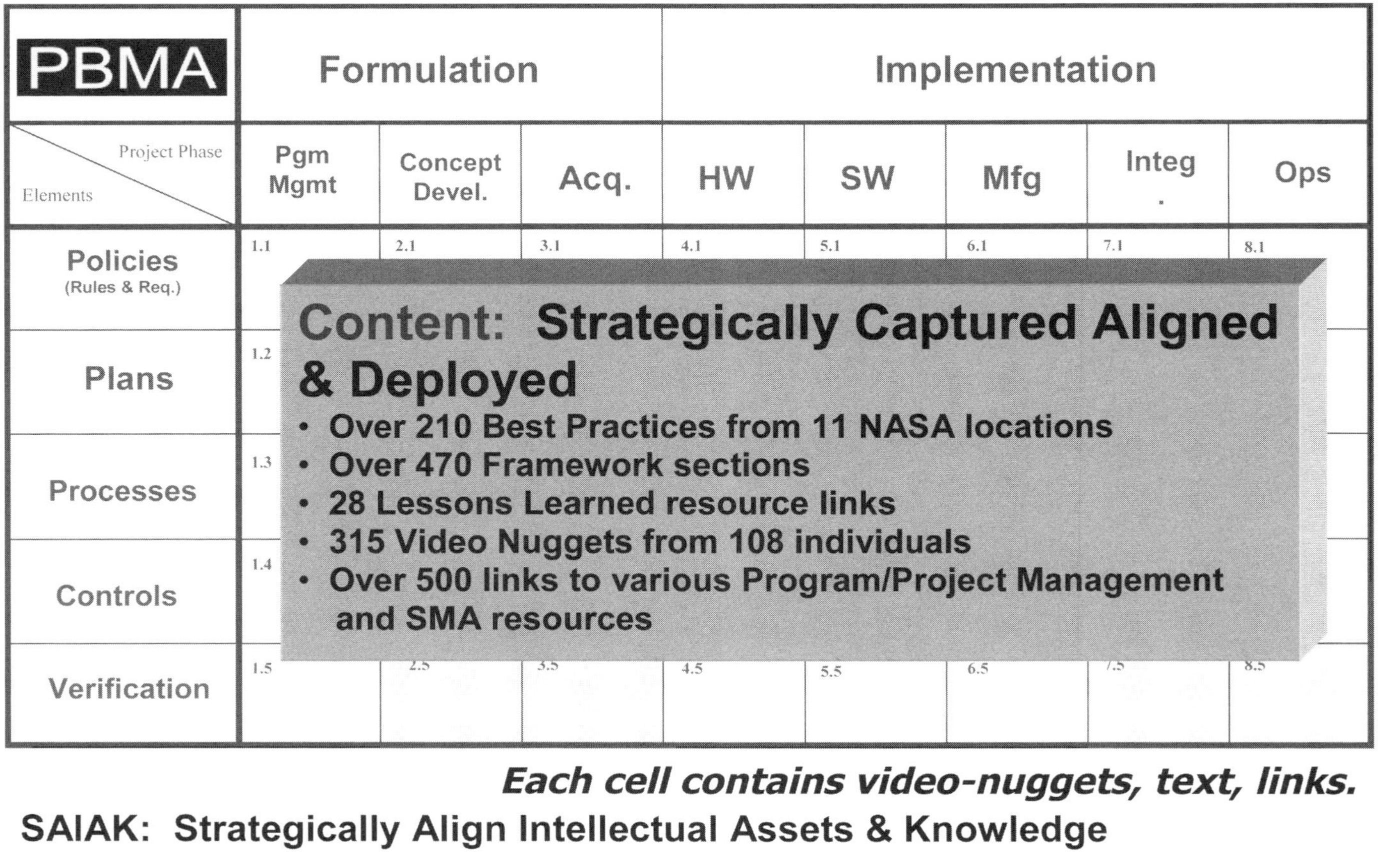

Elements / Project Phase	Formulation			Implementation				
	Pgm Mgmt	Concept Devel.	Acq.	HW	SW	Mfg	Integ	Ops
Policies (Rules & Req.)	1.1	2.1	3.1	4.1	5.1	6.1	7.1	8.1
Plans	1.2							
Processes	1.3							
Controls	1.4							
Verification	1.5	2.5	3.5	4.5	5.5	6.5	7.5	8.5

Content: Strategically Captured Aligned & Deployed

- Over 210 Best Practices from 11 NASA locations
- Over 470 Framework sections
- 28 Lessons Learned resource links
- 315 Video Nuggets from 108 individuals
- Over 500 links to various Program/Project Management and SMA resources

Each cell contains video-nuggets, text, links.

SAIAK: Strategically Align Intellectual Assets & Knowledge

Figure 13.2. Program Management Knowledge Architecture/User Interface

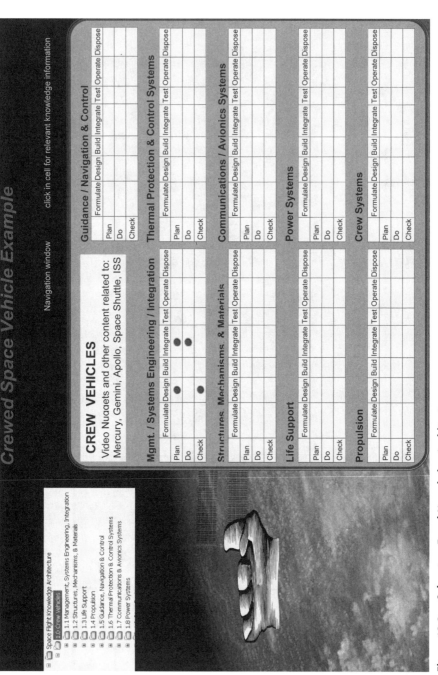

Figure 13.3. Subsystem-Based Knowledge Architecture

environments. The primary concept behind developing this collaborative functionality was to research commercial-off-the-shelf (COTS) products and adapt them to fit within a highly controlled, secure government environment. The latest manifestation of this process is the Enhanced Security Work Group (ESWG). ESWGs provide users with a secure collaborative tool using a validated method of strong user authentication that enables the sharing of information deemed as sensitive/critical data. CoPs, one can argue, reduce travel, reduce email traffic (a critical benefit when sharing very large data files), provide centralized workspace for dispersed/decentralized programs and projects, encourage the sharing of new ideas, and capture and catalog tacit as well as explicit knowledge. Present functionality includes document manager, online calendar, task manager, database manager, web conferencing, discussion forums, announcements, contact directories, email accounts, expense reports, opinion polls, and administration tools.

A second key collaborative functionality is SecureMeeting (SM). SM delivers functionality similar to WebEx, but it is intended for web conferencing situations where shared sensitive data—principally ITAR/EAR, proprietary, and competition-sensitive information—must be protected not only via secure uplinks and downlinks but also on secure servers, ones that reside behind NASA firewalls. SM provides such an enhanced-security, collaborative, online meeting, and web-conferencing solution.

A third collaborative functionality is the Knowledge Registry (KR). The KR is an online "expert finder" database developed to extend the granularity of the NASA Competency Management System (CMS) introducing additional structured fields based on SMA and project work experience to assist in identifying experts to support the program/project or mishap investigation activities. One can also upload credential information, such as transcripts, resumes, biographical sketches, training certifications, papers, and publications. This database, currently searchable only by NASA civil service employees, also contains relevant contractor employee information.

A fourth and emergent collaboration functionality is the implementation of a bounded or fenced wiki infrastructure. Wikis are seen as the natural collaborative complement to the secure CoPs implemented within the framework of the existing agency knowledge management systems. While CoPs deliver a wide range of work group functionality including the means to manage documents the wiki functionality and rule set is uniquely oriented to controlled, change-managed, asynchronous, narrative (document) content development by teams of collaborators.

IT Environment

The PBMA-KMS infrastructure was designed to be flexible, agile, fully scalable, and in alignment and compliance with agency and external enterprise architecture (EA) requirements. In fact, the PBMA-KMS was the first EA-certified KMS at NASA. The approach has been to not lock into a particular technology solution but, in fact, to allow users and content to drive IT requirements. The PBMA-KMS is compliant with NASA's current IT Standards (both security and architectural) and embodies a modular design that can be reconfigured to comply with evolving IT standards (e.g., Windows, IIS, SQL, Section 508), and is capable of being integrated within a "system of systems."

IT Security

The PBMA-KMS has always worked IT security as a part of life cycle management and not just as a one-time milestone. PBMA-KMS conforms to the Glenn Research Center (GRC) IT security requirements for IT security plan, risk assessments, penetration tests, contingency plans, and disaster recovery plans (all plans signed and on file with GRC IT Security). Currently, GRC IT security manages perimeter security from a technical standpoint, for example, ESN, firewalls, and port management. The PBMA-KMS also employs a master IT security plan with subplans developed for each COTS application as required.

IT Reliability

PBMA-KMS has maintained exceptional levels of system availability. In fact, all components of PBMA-KMS have had 100 percent uptime since inception, with the exception of the public website (99.995 percent performance during February 2004). Indeed, it has been user requirements that have driven this "standard" of operational uptime, a standard that has been primarily achieved through extensive design, hardware, and software redundancy.

Return on Investment/Valuation Methods Used

What is the return on investment (ROI) on the email infrastructure at your company? Who last computed the ROI for the natural gas service provided to your business? What is the ROI for the electricity you spend to make a product? After all, plenty of great hand tools are available, and kerosene is pretty inexpensive. As to another perspective, consider the local fire department, Homeland Security, or NASA (or any entity) where manpower, dollars, and time spent on preventing events makes the calculation of a conventional ROI (which would require some method of "counting" events that don't happen—fires, terrorist attacks, mishaps, and so on—a highly problematical and dubious exercise at best). In time the question "What is the ROI for KM?" will go away.

Ultimately it becomes a meaningless question because KM, like security and safety, becomes an essential and critical business service. Wishing to avoid any further irreverent discourse on this topic, the authors wish to assure the reader we will provide some successful quantitative and qualitative metrics to help the reader "play the metrics and ROI game." Figure 13.4 represents a prime example and was the NASA CIO's favorite chart, demonstrating a decreasing user cost with an increasing user base over time—the perfect IT investment dream. Indeed, activity metrics can always be employed.

Examples from early PBMA-KMS development include:

Number of video nuggets online, number in approval, number in production

- Number of best-practice documents online
- Number of active communities of practice
- Number of members
- Number of links to lessons-learned case studies
- Number of documented testimonials
- Initial rollout briefings and workshops conducted at X field centers
- Number of participants in rollout events
- Anticipated time savings for functionality in development
- Recognition (letters and certificates) for X individuals supporting design, development, and implementation
- Number of strategic partnerships with NASA organizations, academic institions, voluntary professional, and standards organizations
- Number of presentations at conferences

The quantitative metrics game has also been played with often dubious assumptions concerning "time saved" per visit or per return visit, assuming hourly rates, duration of visits, and number of visitors. In particular, collaborative tools are noted for their ability to save time and money by reducing travel, providing centralized workspaces and managing version control of group documents. We have all seen the laborious arithmetic gymnastics associated with these "cost-savings analyses," which may appeal to certain accountants and managers. Instead, we submit that the CEO should look at what is happening within their organization using quantitative/qualitative "metric pictures" like figure 13.5, the authors' favorite. Here the message is qualitative—people are starting to integrate/communicate across organizational and geographic boundaries in a collaborative way—breaking down stovepipe behaviors so often criticized in dysfunctional organizations. Also figure 13.6, another favorite, shows the increase in communities and overall membership in communities over a six-year period.

NASA ROI EXAMPLE

Defining Success:

- **Validated Requirements** – The acceptance by the user community and the continued growth of all functional areas shows that the **PBMA** solution is aligned with the needs of our customers
- **Managed Growth** – The steady build punctuated by the rise in FY05 demonstrates the ability of the PBMA system to maintain its relevance and continue to provide exceptional performance (99.995% uptime)
- **IT Stewardship** – PBMA has cost effectively managed the program through the product lifecycle and continues to relieve pressure on Agency Missions by providing well-managed IT services.

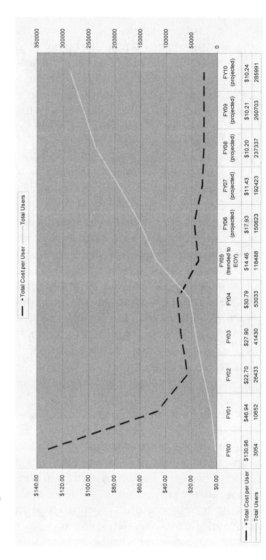

	FY00	FY01	FY02	FY03	FY04	FY05 (trended to EOY)	FY06 (projected)	FY07 (projected)	FY08 (projected)	FY09 (projected)	FY10 (projected)
Total Cost per User	$130.98	$46.94	$22.70	$27.90	$30.79	$14.46	$17.93	$11.43	$10.20	$10.21	$10.24
Total Users	3054	10652	26433	41430	53033	118488	150623	192423	237337	260703	285991

Legend: - - Total Cost per User ——— Total Users

Figure 13.4. "Perfection" Metric for IT Investments

PBMA CoPs—Tearing Down the Walls/Geographical Barriers

- **NASA is traditionally organized by Center**
- **Center-specific stovepipes are an unfortunate by-product of this organizational structure**
- **CoPs allow the users to tear down the walls and operate as a singular entity – focused on common objectives (>60% of the communities in PBMA are supporting multiple centers)**

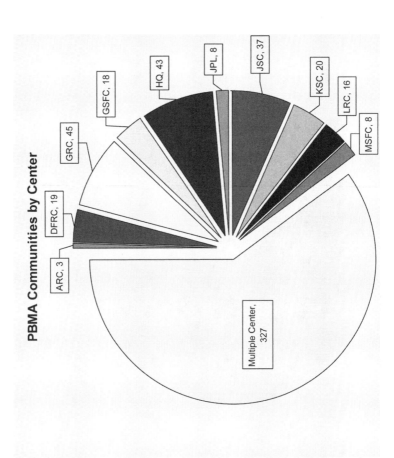

PBMA Communities by Center

ARC, 3
DFRC, 19
GRC, 45
GSFC, 18
HQ, 43
JPL, 8
JSC, 37
KSC, 20
LRC, 16
MSFC, 8
Multiple Center, 327

Figure 13.5. Evidence of KM Bringing Value

PBMA CoPs – From There to Here

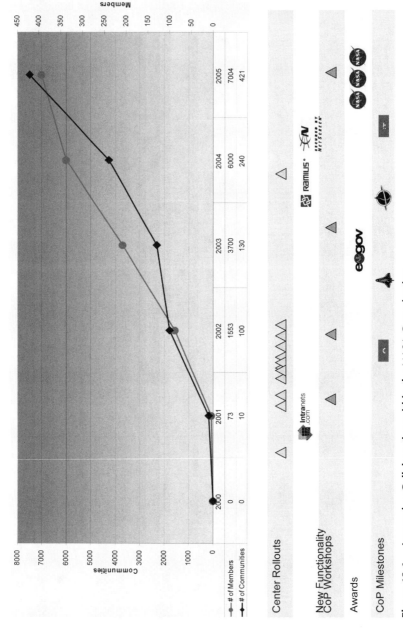

	2000	2001	2002	2003	2004	2005
# of Members	0	73	1553	3700	6000	7004
# of Communities	0	10	100	130	240	421

Figure 13.6. Increasing Collaboration within the NASA Organization

WHAT ACTUALLY HAPPENED WITH THE PROJECT

The acceptance by the user community and the continued growth of all functional areas shows that PBMA-KMS solutions are aligned with the needs of the customers. The steady build punctuated by the rise in FY05 demonstrates the ability of the PBMA-KMS to maintain its relevance and continue to provide exceptional performance (99.995 percent uptime). The PBMA-KMS management team has cost effectively managed the program through its initial product life cycle and continues to relieve pressure on agency missions and support functions by providing well-managed and readily accessed IT services. As a result, PBMA-KMS received the 2003 eGov Pioneer Award for "Outstanding e-Government Best Practice as an application that has streamlined operations and improved government services." Other awards included the 2004 NASA HQ Honor Award: Civil Servant/Contractor Achievement Award, and the 2005 GRC Honor Award: Civil Servant/Contractor Achievement Award for "Outstanding support to Columbia Accident Investigation Board and NASA's Columbia Task Force."

In 2005 the PBMA-KMS management team received the NASA Agency Honor Award, NASA's most prestigious, approved by the administrator and presented to a number of carefully selected individuals and groups, both government and nongovernmental, who have distinguished themselves by making outstanding contributions to the agency's mission.

In addition, on April 7, 2005, the PBMA-KMS became the first KM system at NASA to become fully certified to enterprise architectural standards (see figure 13.7), affirming and documenting linkage with mission and customer requirements, management due diligence, rigorous resource planning, demonstrated use of metrics, implementation of an investment and cost-recovery approach, implementation of risk-management processes, compliance with IT security requirements, and alignment with the Federal Enterprise Architectural Reference Model.

SUCCESSES AND FAILURES: LESSONS LEARNED

Perhaps the best approach to summarizing "successes and failures" can be provided in the form of a series of short and succinct lessons learned. These can be effectively grouped into four basic categories as described below. It should also be noted that many of these lessons learned can also trace their origins to our initial developmental concepts: a practical and practiced application of KM theory, following basic systems engineering principles and practices, and adopting a continuous-improvement/risk-management philosophy.

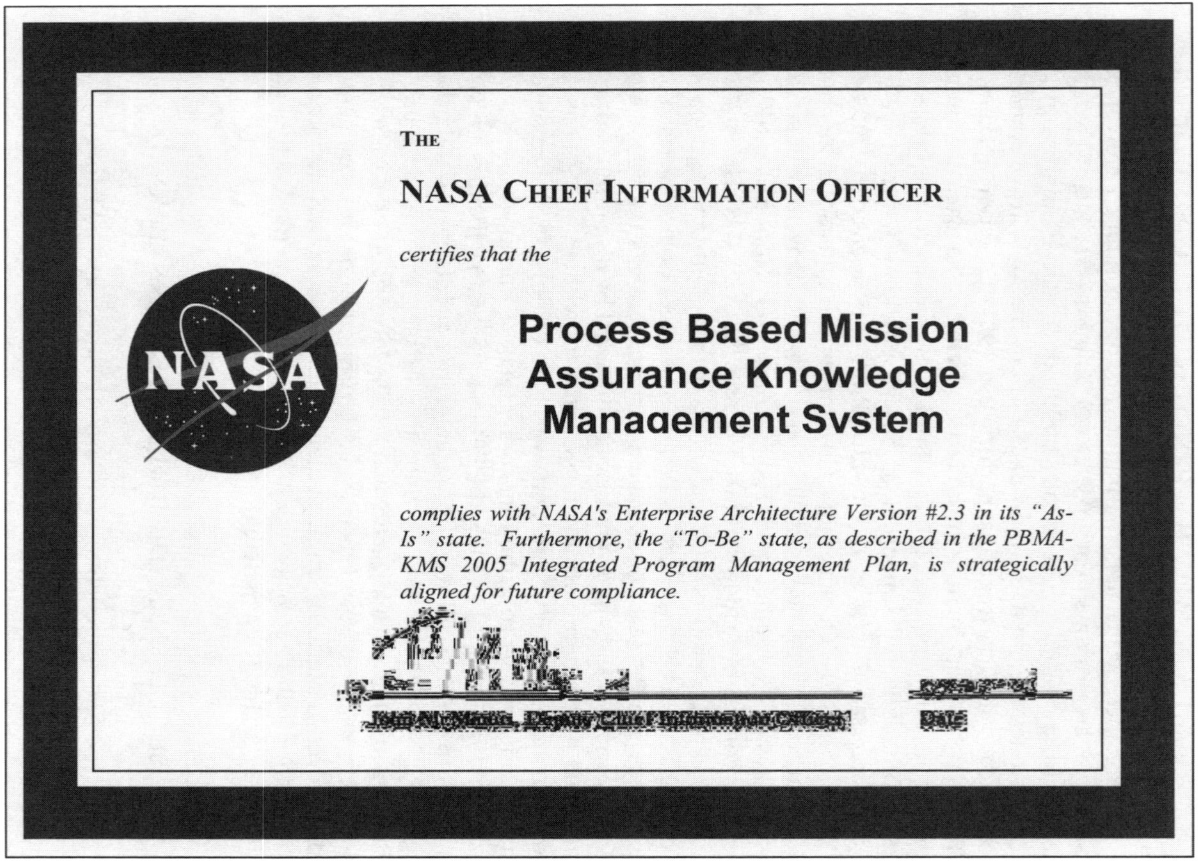

THE

NASA CHIEF INFORMATION OFFICER

certifies that the

Process Based Mission Assurance Knowledge Management System

complies with NASA's Enterprise Architecture Version #2.3 in its "As-Is" state. Furthermore, the "To-Be" state, as described in the PBMA-KMS 2005 Integrated Program Management Plan, is strategically aligned for future compliance.

Figure 13.7. Enterprise Architectural Certification

Leadership

- Get a knowledge or K-vision . . . a going-in knowledge architectural construct.
- Tie the K-vision to (or the vision should reflect) the corporate "knitting" or core competency. The goal is to help people perform the core function more efficiently and effectively.
- Sell the vision to a powerful business unit sponsor with his/her own budget. "God bless the child that's got his own."
- "Mind the knitting"—keep focused.
- Develop appropriate metrics (activity and results-based) to manage the inevitable ROI questions.
- Involve management with implementation actions.
- Tie in to every available political toehold.

Organization

- Use an existing distributed organizational structure as an advocate network.
- Forge partnerships with CIO/IT, security, and external-affairs organizations. Find out what it takes to keep them happy. Build and operate the KMS on the basis of "compliance by design." Build the KMS within their constraints. Incorporate security measures as required—it actually enhances and strengthens the value of the KMS.
- Partner with a formal training organization.
- Partner with the formal systems engineering organization. Incorporate their needs and objectives—demonstrate synergy.

Technology

- Use available organization IT infrastructure.
- Drive evolution of infrastructure to the extent possible.
- Create your own infrastructure when necessary to move beyond organizational inertia. (Note: Organizational managed IT infrastructures change slowly. Focus is on perceived "economies of scale" and standardization. The need to satisfy multiple, often disparate and unconnected customer requirements slows everything down.)
- Use COTS hardware/software when it makes sense. COTS will almost always be way ahead of big, bureaucratic organizational technology.
- Remember that the www is the ultimate infrastructure.

Culture / Customers / Communities

- Establish "champions" at each facility across the organization or enterprise.
- Conduct formal—well-staffed and funded—rollout at each facility.

- Follow-up with hands-on training/workshops, which facilitates customer/user feedback.
- Conduct annual workshops/symposia bringing together all champions.
- Develop banners, posters, updated handout materials.
- Recognize and reward performance.

Content and Functionality

- Unlike real estate, in KM only *six* things matter: Content, content, content, and functionality, functionality, functionality.
- Stay on top of content—keep it fresh and relevant.
- Listen to your customers—give them functionality they need and want and use.
- Optimize access—keep as much as possible in the public domain.

EPILOGUE

Much has been accomplished but much remains ahead for the NASA PBMA-KMS managers and other agency officials. Consider the following:

Additional emphasis on tacit knowledge capture: With a continuing brain drain as NASA baby boomers retire it is imperative that the PBMA-KMS management team expand partnership with the CIO and Human Capitol Resource Management to launch a major video nugget and story-telling acquisition project over the next several years to identify, interview, and record retiring experts in critical technology and management areas.

Expanded use of Knowledge Registry (KR): Initially conceived as a tool to facilitate SMA audit teams, independent assessments, and mishap investigations, KR will have major and critical relevance to NASA's future workforce balancing activities.

Updated user interfaces: Continued development of alternative user interface knowledge architectures will provide users with choice (a pull-down menu) of how to access their knowledge artifacts depending upon the task or work activity on a given day.

Compliance Verification Information System (CVIS): With increased emphasis on formal and structured compliance verification activities in the post *Columbia* era, the agency's SMA and program/project communities will benefit from continuing development of the CVIS functionality (including audit schedules, planning, audit findings, and trending analyses) being established within the PBMA-KMS framework.

Wikis: Effective critical decision (CD) forums are key to program success. A proposed CD-Wiki will drive the narrative synthesis of complex risk issues into a holistic picture with a bottom line. Implementing the CD-Wiki will sharpen the argument of forum presenters and the thinking of all participants. The CD-Wiki will enable asynchronous collaboration—allowing thinking and broad opinion "to brew," iterate, and improve with input and ideas from a diverse cross-stovepipe set of experts afforded access to the decision forum. Further, the CD-Wiki provides instantaneous drill-down to the supporting evidence, providing a complete and integrated package rather than a fragmented story. Finally, the CD-Wiki would create a complete historical record of decision, documenting all changes in position and in the case of failures provide a preassembled and organized package of decisions, decision rationale, and supporting data for mishap review teams.

The NASA Safety Center: In mid-2007 NASA is establishing a NASA Safety Center (NSC) located at Glenn Research Center. The PBMA-KMS will be folded into the newly established organization and integrated into a "system of systems" designed to provide specialized services to the agency's program/project and safety and mission assurance communities. While the name may change, it is anticipated that the core PBMA-KMS vision, concept, and functionality will continue to support NASA-wide collaboration, organizational learning, safety, and mission success.

REFERENCES

Baldanza, C., and M. Stankosky. 2000. "Knowledge Management: An Evolutionary Architecture Toward Enterprise Engineering," INCOSE, March.

Calabrese, Frank. n.d. "A Suggested Framework of Key Elements Defining Effective Enterprise-Wide Knowledge Management Programs." Abstract of dissertation, George Washington University.

Newman, J. Steven. 1997. "Life Cycle Risk Management Elements for NASA Programs: A Program Manager's Guide to Faster/Better and Cheaper." NASA Office of Safety & Mission Assurance, June.

———. 2002. "The Knowledge Path to Mission Success: Overview of the NASA Process-Based Mission Assurance Knowledge Management System," Reliability and Maintainability Symposium (RAMS), Seattle, WA, January 28–31.

———. 2005a. "PBMA-KMS Strategies for Thriving KM Programs: KM Myth-Busting, Space Shuttles, and Reindeer Tracking, Tales from the Front Lines of Knowledge Management." eGov 2005 Conference, April 21, Washington, DC.

———. 2005b. "PBMA-KMS: NASA's IT Systems and Enterprise Architecture: The Present and the Future." Presentation to the NASA Small Business Solutions Conference, September 2, New York.

Newman, J. Steven, and Stephen M. Wander. 2005. "The Development of the PBMA-KMS: How We Did It." Presentation to GSA, December, Washington, DC.

———. 2006. "KM for Improved Decision-Making and Program Management: A Pioneering Public Sector KM Case Study." eGov 2006 Conference, April 19, Washington, DC.

Stankosky, M., ed. 2004. *Creating the Discipline of Knowledge Management: The Latest in University Research.* Boston: Butterworth-Heinemann.

Wander, Stephen M. 2006. "The Evolution of Communities of Practice in NASA's Diverse Business Environment." Session 2-6, Strategies to Integrate Communities of Practice into Business Operations, eGov Conference, April 21, Washington, DC.

14

Leveraging Knowledge at AARP

Jody Holtzman

Larry Prusak's definition of Knowledge Management (KM) has been a good reference point for KM for many years—to provide "the right information to the right people in the right context at the right time."

At AARP, we have an additional mantra that guides our KM activities: "To create, share, and leverage knowledge."

Most discussions of KM, and competitive intelligence (CI) for that matter, have focused on process. In the case of knowledge management this has involved discussions about sharing knowledge: the process by which we collect it, make it accessible, and get it to the right people. In the case of CI, here too much of the discussion is focused on the collection of intelligence and the creation of intelligence networks, and the research and elicitation techniques required to obtain the missing piece of the puzzle.

This focus on process has led to extensive discussions (and a multimillion dollar business) about the question "How?" How do we obtain and get information and knowledge to the people who need it? As a result, much of the discussion has focused on the technologies that enable this knowledge sharing and dissemination.

The fact is, the process issues are essential if an organization is to truly benefit from the knowledge created within its walls, let alone obtained from external sources and explorations. However, as the old saying goes, "garbage in, garbage out."

The challenge at AARP and most organizations involves a preceding over-riding question, which in turn begs several additional questions. The overriding question is this: How do we leverage knowledge across the organization?

- How do we create the "right" knowledge?
- How do we understand the context?
- How do we design our research and analysis so that it provides need-to-have insight?
- How do we communicate our insights so they are actionable and inform the goals and decision making of our internal client(s)?

This chapter will address these questions and provide examples of how we are dealing with them at AARP.

KNOWLEDGE MANAGEMENT AT AARP

Knowledge Management at AARP is both an organization and a way of doing things.

Organizational Structure: The Knowledge Management group at AARP is responsible for research and strategic analysis of issues that affect our ability to achieve AARP's social impact and member value goals. The group is organized into six departments with the following responsibilities:

- **National Member Research**—Conducts nationwide research on the needs, opinions, and interests of AARP members and potential members. This unit conducts national member tracking surveys on awareness, use, and satisfaction with AARP's programs and services; research to support member service, recruitment, and retention; research to support AARP's branding efforts; and editorial tracking research for AARP's key publications, *AARP the Magazine* and the *AARP Bulletin.*
- **State Member Research**—Provides research support for AARP's state presence in fifty states and three territories with a special focus on the needs, interests, concerns, and opinions of our members. State Member Research designs and conducts surveys or evaluations to support planning, advocacy, and/or education efforts.
- **Strategic Issues Research**—Provides research expertise on association-wide strategic policy issues. This department's goal is to provide actionable research that helps the association understand the views of its members and the population at large about the policy issues of the day so that AARP can better serve our members.

- **Environmental Analysis**—Provides information about the external and internal environment in which we provide service to our members. It provides tools and information to staff and volunteers to support their planning and decision making. These services include demographic analysis, geodemographic analysis and maps, environmental scanning, trend analysis, economic forecasting, and operational evaluation.
- **Strategic Analysis and Intelligence**—Provides actionable, timely insight about our evolving competitive environment and assesses the implications of these changing external environmental dynamics for achieving AARP's social impact and member value agendas and business goals. In addition to our effort to learn about rival activities, organizations, and companies, Strategic Analysis and Intelligence uses the "lens of the competitor" to better understand and meet the needs of our members and prospective members, so that AARP can successfully serve them, attract and retain new members, and become an even more effective membership organization.
- **Research Information Center (Library)**—Delivers the timely targeted information AARP staff need to better understand the interests and concerns of the members they serve and to support the strategic and business activities of the association. It accomplishes this through its extensive library collection on social gerontology, management, technology, and other related topics; customized database searches; answering reference questions and connecting staff with resources; and loaning, subscribing to, and purchasing materials for staff. The library also provides access to an array of resources through its electronic services.

Making Knowledge Accessible: Each of the departments in the AARP Knowledge Management group provides support to clients across the association. The work that is conducted typically is for either an internal audience and purpose or an external audience. Work conducted for internal audiences typically has minimal circulation, often limited to the requesting client.

Work conducted with the purpose of serving external audiences has much greater circulation and is made accessible to AARP staff on the organization's intranet, as well as our website www.AARP.org.

Knowledge Management makes available two categories of information:

- One page on the intranet lists the Knowledge Management Research Agenda for Public Release. This lets staff across the association know what work is being planned or initiated. It is updated every few days and includes both due dates for completion and a contact person in Knowledge Management, typically the project manager overseeing the work.
- The second page on the intranet that makes our work available and accessible is called Policy and Research. This page includes links to all of

KM's work that is publicly available for downloading. A dedicated team in KM's Research Information Center (our library) has responsibility for posting all publicly available research reports produced by Knowledge Management, as well as policy analyses produced by our colleagues in AARP's Public Policy Institute.

Lastly, Knowledge Management, as well as most other groups across AARP, maintains a variety of internally "public" folders on an internal V-Drive. This work is organized by subject area and often includes work papers as well as final reports.

The net result of these channels is easy-to-access information about our members—their needs, preferences, and desires as well as analyses of the policy issues affecting them.

THE KM-CI CHALLENGE AT AARP

The KM and CI challenge facing AARP is the classic one facing most large, multidivisional organizations. That is, how to leverage knowledge across organizational silos.

The obvious part of this challenge is organizational, and we illustrate how we have addressed this below. But before addressing this structural element, it is also important to realize that another part of the challenge at AARP and elsewhere is definitional—what orientation to bring to the conduct of competitive intelligence, market and other research, and knowledge management, and how these functions are internally defined.

Assumptions, Definitions, and AARP Differences

Assumptions: The Knowledge Management group at AARP starts with the assumption that while different disciplines such as competitive intelligence and analysis, and member and market research have different elements that they focus on, they fundamentally are types of research with a common objective—to provide forward-looking, timely, actionable insight about all facets of the external environment that create opportunities and threats that can potentially affect our ability to achieve our social mission, strategy, and business objectives.

Another assumption that we have is that unless the insight is linked, used, and incorporated into the decision-making process by senior management, it simply will be nice-to-know information, rather than timely, need-to-have, value adding, actionable insight.

Definitions: In most companies there is an implicit definitional separation between competitive intelligence and market research that walls-off the examination of companies from customers and prospective customers. What is lost in this artificial separation is the fact that CI stands for *competitive* intelligence, not *company* intelligence. And nowhere in the phrase "market research" does the word "customer" appear.

The fact is each of these disciplines aims to illuminate the competitive marketplace. However, the competitive market can only be understood through the integration and analysis of research and intelligence about *all* the elements influencing the dynamic marketplace, supply *and* demand. To be sure, there is a need to understand the constituent parts that comprise and influence the competitive marketplace. And, yes, this often involves a "deep dive" on a particular company or customer segment.

However, even when such a deep dive is conducted, it should not be done in an isolated, unconnected way. Unfortunately, this is exactly what happens all too often and typically. Unconnected company profiles are created in the CI group and complemented by unconnected customer research in the market research group. Adding insult to injury, market research managers typically do not read the company profiles and the CI group doesn't read the customer research. You have little chance of connecting all the dots if you don't look at them.

The competitive market in any industry is about one thing—multiple companies trying to get customers/clients to buy from them and not the other guys. This is what the competition is about—acquiring customers. As a famous rabbi once said, "the rest is commentary."

And to answer the central question that enables your company to acquire customers—that is, why should anyone buy from us and not our competitors?—you need to understand the needs and preferences of customers on the one hand, and the intentions and capabilities of competitors to meet those customer needs and preferences on the other. The only way to gain this understanding is by integrating and synthesizing competitive intelligence and market research. The synergy that is achieved is "customer-centric market intelligence"—an understanding of the market that is greater than the sum of its parts.

AARP differences: At AARP, as a nonprofit organization we have an important difference compared with for-profit organizations. The key difference is the role and focus of our social-impact goals and the achievement of what we call "the triple bottom line." In addition to the typical financial top line and bottom line measures, our efforts in a given market also must achieve particular social-impact measures.

When AARP enters a market and decides to offer a product or service, its goal is to either create a market in order to address a particular social need of the fifty-plus population or to raise the bar and consumer standards within a given product or service market. This orientation was embedded in

AARP by its founder, Dr. Ethel Percy Andrus, with her initial effort to provide health insurance for retired teachers at a time when not a single insurance company would provide such coverage due to the perceived risk of serving retirees.

Another very important difference is our view of "competitors." Unlike for-profit companies whose competitive goal is greater and greater market share and ultimately monopoly, AARP's success is dependent on other players following our lead—either by entering a market we have created, as with health insurance for retired teachers or Medicare supplemental insurance, or copying the higher standards we set, as with mutual fund prospectuses written in plain English and sold by salaried employees without commission-based incentives, as occurs in our subsidiary AARP Financial Inc.

These differences provide the context for the research and external environmental analysis conducted in the Knowledge Management group. Everything we do is designed to inform and help achieve the long-term and short-term objectives required to meet our social mission. As such, our research and analysis informs each and all of the elements in the cycle shown in figure 14.1.

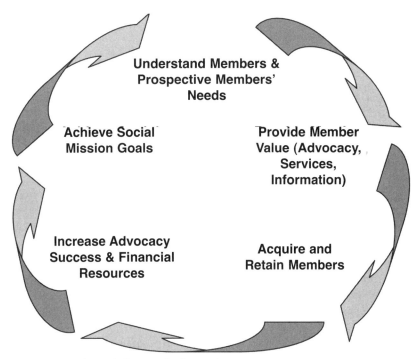

Figure 14.1. Informed Elements in the Cycle

THE SOLUTION AT AARP

Organizational Solutions

Even with a holistic orientation, organizational structure can be an obstacle to holistic analysis, discussion, and insights. Organizational silos get in the way of reaching out across existing boundaries to obtain the critical and knowledgeable insights of those viewing a given market or environment from different vantage points.

In the AARP Knowledge Management group two organizational changes have been designed and implemented to address the problem of silo-confined knowledge.

The first was the establishment of Research Integration groups with a focus on four key association-wide priority goals: healthcare, economic and retirement security, member value, and the AARP brand. The organization chart (figure 14.2) illustrates the players from each of the KM departments that are now at the table and the areas of responsibility that each group has. The goals of this new organizational structure are to:

- Break down the silos
- Bring people together who have worked on common issue/subject areas
- Identify what we know and don't know
- Create a space that enables cross-silo, holistic discussion from multiple perspectives on a given issue/subject
- Create centers of knowledge on key issue areas for the association

The second organizational change concerns the role of research librarians in KM's Research Information Center. Historically, reference librarians have played a largely reactive role, responding to requests for information from across the association. Recently, we concluded that in order to raise the level of value provided to clients, we needed to strengthen the organizational relationships between the librarians and key clients.

The selection of these "key clients" was driven by the association's goals and the owners of those goals. As a result, we now have a new "embedded librarian" model, whereby a librarian has a couple of clients to whom they are attached with the goal of becoming an intrinsic member of that client's team. By doing so, the assumption is that these librarians will become increasingly knowledgeable about the client's short-term and longer-term goals and the information needs that these engender. In this way, librarians can be more proactive and anticipate their client's needs for information and insight.

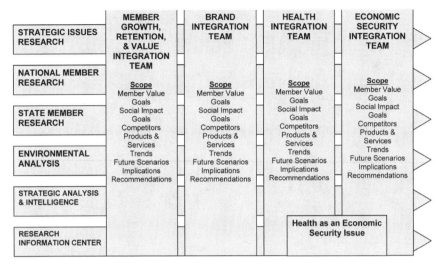

Figure 14.2. Organization Chart

Analytic Solutions

The benefit of removing the organizational and analytic barriers is a stronger understanding of the customer and market—or in the case of AARP, our members and the external environment. This doesn't change the fact that different disciplines have a different focus on a particular piece of the market, that is, companies on the one hand and members/consumers on the other. As such, different questions are posed with regard to each.

For example, competitive intelligence managers will ask questions such as:

- What are our rivals' strategies and plans?
- What would prompt a change of strategy and plans?
- What are our rivals' strengths and weaknesses?
- What accounts for their successes and defeats?
- How are other organizations/companies organized?
- How might they reorganize and why?
- What pressures are other organizations and companies facing, internally and externally?
- How might our objectives be influenced by the pressures facing our rivals?
- How well will other organizations/companies fare in alternative scenarios of the future market environment?
- Which rivals pose a threat to us, now and in the future?

Researchers on the other hand will ask questions such as:

- How will the needs of our members affect the future shape of different markets?
- What do our members need?
- What do our members want?
- What do our members value?
- What are the preferences of our members?
- What is our brand reputation and image with our members?
- Which member segments present the greatest opportunity for our products and services?
- What do members think about our new product/service?
- Do we have the right messaging to "speak to" the needs and preferences of our members?

A host of business decisions require the combined efforts and integrated market insights of both CI and research in providing to senior management the various elements of the market and external environment. And although each type of research may answer particular questions, it is the synergistic insight that is key for many decisions—the combined insight that is greater than the sum of its parts. In addressing these business decisions, the synergy between competitive intelligence and research lies in part with the *integrative questions*. These are the questions with which you use the lens of the customer to understand your competitors, and the lens of the competitor to understand your customers—in AARP's case, our members. Such business decisions and their respective integrative questions include, but are not limited to, those shown in table 14.1.

Each of these business decisions requires a combination of different types of research and analysis that are conducted, respectively, by competitive intelligence and research functions. Neither can answer the questions alone in a way that will effectively support senior management's requirements for actionable intelligence. And although it is possible to derive answers at the end of two separate, parallel research processes conducted independently by each function, much greater insight and efficiencies will be gained by organizing these efforts together on the front end of the effort.

KNOWLEDGE MANAGEMENT AND
ACHIEVING SYNERGY BETWEEN CI AND RESEARCH

So what are some of the practical steps to attain synergy between CI and market research? First of all, break down the silos! It is of prime importance to do this in support of particular business decisions like those above. However,

Table 14.1. Business Decisions and Their Respective Integrative Questions

Business Decision	Integrative Questions
New product development and launch	• Which member needs and preferences are not being met by AARP or by others in the market? • What do other orgs/companies assume about our members and prospective members?
New market entry	• Which markets and member segments are other orgs/companies targeting? • What do our members think of us versus others in the market?
Positioning and value proposition development (enterprise and new products/services)	• How well do our members and potential members believe we fulfill their needs and preferences as compared with others in the market?
Market opportunity identification	• Which member needs and preferences are not being met by AARP or by others in the market? • What are our rivals' assumptions about the market ?
Marketing/ad messaging	• Which value propositions—ours and our rivals'—resonate most with our members? • How does our messaging differentiate us from others'?
Merger & acquisition decisions	• Which org/company would strengthen our ability to serve our members?

the general rule should be, wherever you sit organizationally, you must reach out across the organizational boundaries to obtain the critical and knowledgeable eye of those viewing the market from different vantage points.

This is not limited only to CI and market research. It should include strategic planning, R&D, public relations, human resources, investor relations, even finance. However, at a minimum, CI and research units must work together, both in designing research and analyzing the results and their implications for strategic decision making.

At AARP, we are beginning to achieve this through our Research Integration Teams, which bring together CI and all of the researchers who have experience in a given topical area of high importance to the organization.

In addition to pulling together ad hoc teams for particular decision support projects, two activities can be easily initiated on an ongoing basis without any cost. First, a common CI-Research calendar can identify the focus, scope, purpose, and timing of research projects and the use of outside research firms. If requests for proposals (RFPs) have been produced, they can be posted on the calendar. Second, the lens of the customer should be incorporated into competitor analysis and the lens of the competitor into consumer research and customer satisfaction and loyalty surveys. This is a way to examine the integrative questions that link competitors and customers.

The job of CI is to obtain help from Research to put the customer/member at the center of competitor profiling and competitive analysis. The result—higher likelihood of identifying key areas of competitive advantage and weakness among competitors and your company regarding the needs and preferences of the customer.

The job of Research is to obtain help from the CI group to embed questions about the company *and* competitors into all relevant member/customer research, for example, customer satisfaction and loyalty, product and market needs and preference assessments, brand positioning, marketing messaging, and so on. The result—a deeper understanding of how member/customer needs and preferences are defined and fulfilled by both an organization and its rivals/competitors, which in turn should help identify areas of advantage, opportunity, and concern.

CONCLUSION

Decision makers need only one thing from CI and research and the leveraging through knowledge management of the insights they produce—and that is value-added insight. The job of knowledge management at AARP is to create, share, and leverage knowledge. Our focus going forward is on the latter, which is in many ways the most challenging. Through both organizational changes and a new orientation to both our analysis and the communication of our findings, we are finding that while difficult, these are goals embraced across the organization and motivated by the knowledge that our efforts directly support the mission of AARP—AARP is dedicated to enhancing quality of life for all as we age.

Index

Note: *Italic* page numbers indicate illustrations.

About the Editor and Contributors

ABOUT THE EDITOR

Jay Liebowitz is a professor in the Carey Business School at Johns Hopkins University.

ABOUT THE CONTRIBUTORS

Rajeev Bali is subgroup leader and reader for Knowledge Management for Healthcare at Coventry University in the United Kingdom.

Kimiz Dalkir is assistant professor in the Graduate School of Information Studies at McGill University in Montreal.

Ashish Dwivedi is a lecturer in information sciences at the Centre for System Studies at the University of Hull in the United Kingdom.

Colleen Elliott is the director of knowledge management at Catholic Health Initiatives in Denver, Colorado.

Steve Goldberg is president of INET International, Inc., in Ontario, Canada.

Joy Goldman is director of leadership and organizational development at St. Joseph Medical Center in Towson, Maryland.

Jody Holtzman is director of strategic analysis and knowledge management at AARP in Washington, D.C.

Sandra Hom is a research associate at the Naval Postgraduate School in Monterey, California.

Tom Housel is a professor at the Naval Postgraduate School in Monterey, California.

Thomas E. Kern was senior associate for knowledge management at the Annie E. Casey Foundation in Baltimore. He is currently vice president of member services at the Intelligent Transportation Society of America.

Denise Lee is senior consultant for PricewaterhouseCoopers in McLean, Virginia.

Laura Moore is director of knowledge management in the Office of Applied Science, Public Building Service, General Services Administration, in Washington, D.C.

Johnathan Mun is a professor at the Naval Postgraduate School in Monterey, California.

J. Steven Newman is vice president for technology applications at ARES Corporation in Arlington, Virginia.

Eduardo Rodriguez was EDC knowledge management advisor at Export Development Canada in Ottawa, Canada. He is now president of IQ Analytics in Canada.

Eric Tarantino is a research associate at the Naval Postgraduate School in Monterey, California.

Stephen M. Wander is senior aerospace engineer in the Office of Safety and Mission Assurance at NASA Headquarters in Washington, D.C.

Nilmini Wickramasinghe is with the Center for the Management of Medical Technology in the Stuart School of Business at the Illinois Institute of Technology in Chicago.